Your Money — Uncommon Insights*

*What you *REALLY* need to know to protect and enhance your wealth!

By Joe Biegel, CFP®, J.D.

All rights reserved. No part of this book shall be reproduced or transmitted in any form or by any means, electronic, mechanical, magnetic, photographic including photocopying, recording or by any information storage and retrieval system, without prior written permission of the author. No patent liability is assumed with respect to the use of the information contained herein. Although every precaution has been taken in the preparation of this book, the publisher and author assume no responsibility for errors or omissions. Neither is any liability assumed for damages resulting from the use of the information contained herein.

The information contained in this book is intended for educational, background and food for thought purposes and is not financial, legal, tax, accounting or any other type of professional advice. Further, as I hope is made clear throughout this book, the information presented here is not intended to be used in lieu of expert professional advice; for that, you should seek the assistance of a properly qualified professional. The author, the publisher, and their employees, agents and other representatives are not liable for any damages relating to the use of this book or the reliance on any information contained herein.

Copyright © 2011 by Joe Biegel, CFP®, J.D.
First Edition

ISBN 0-7414-6640-6

Printed in the United States of America

Published May 2011

INFINITY PUBLISHING
1094 New DeHaven Street, Suite 100
West Conshohocken, PA 19428-2713
Toll-free (877) BUY BOOK
Local Phone (610) 941-9999
Fax (610) 941-9959
Info@buybooksontheweb.com
www.buybooksontheweb.com

To my three girls: the source of many
other uncommon insights!

Table of Contents

Introduction	1
Money Profile Quiz	5
Laying The Foundation: **Protecting Your Money**	
1. Money and Creditors	9
2. Money and Sickness	17
3. Money and Death	29
4. Money and Life (Insurance, that is)	41
Building The Structure: **Growing Your Money**	
5. Money and Headwinds	59
6. Money and Savings	67
7. Money and Growth	71
Capping It Off: **Using Your Money**	
8. Money and Its Use	93
9. Money and Legacy	111
Epilogue: Choosing Help	117

Introduction

Several years ago a family friend, 40 years old, died suddenly. He was a successful small business owner with a wife and three very young children. His death devastated the family emotionally – that was unavoidable. **What was avoidable was the financial devastation and havoc the family experienced.** At the core of their trouble was that the husband/father (who was very self-confident, like many small business owners) had no intention of dying for a very long time! Thus, he had almost no life insurance, no real investment strategy (his business was his sole investment), no plans for how his family would continue the business after his death, and on and on. The result was that the business fell apart, the wife had to sell the house, move across the country with her children to live with her parents, and basically start all over.

There are many, many folks in more or less the same precarious position as this family, either because they haven't taken the steps to prepare themselves for the unexpected (e.g., premature death) or for the expected (e.g., retirement). That is not due to an insufficient *quantity* of information – the media is full of it. I've read countless books on personal finance and, frankly and frustratingly, none are particularly helpful - a few have some useful tidbits but **what's missing is *quality* information that provides a comprehensive, logical and integrated strategy that readily can be followed by busy professionals**. As a result, even in the case of those who are inclined to take the steps our friend did not, most people either don't adequately address their finances or, like weight-loss, do so by grabbing at a quick-fix, one-dimensional idea (for instance, the vast majority of those books I mentioned focus only on "investing" and "investments", and you'll learn in this book why that's just a piece of what matters). Thus, I felt compelled to fill this gap.

My goal is to help you protect the money you have, grow as much more of it as optimally possible and give you the ability to get the most use out of it possible. As a result, you and your loved ones will be secure no matter which way the future winds blow, which should significantly enhance your economic confidence.

Although this book does contain a number of facts and details, it is by no stretch of the imagination a "do it yourself" book or "financial planning for dummies." I often tell clients that what I do isn't rocket science and that all of them are smart enough to do it themselves – but almost no one does. Why? Because they don't have the time, interest or tools – and usually all three. While this book isn't intended to give you any of those things, it IS intended to give someone who knows she should be doing more with her[1] finances sufficient motivation to take the next step. That motivation may come from a variety of sources – fear, opportunity, responsibility, and maybe even greed. Any of those will do!

To achieve all this book lays out, you're going to need help. I know it sounds self-serving for me as a financial professional to say this, but I knew it to be the case even when I was the client on the other side of the table. Again, I say this not because you CAN'T do it yourself but because you WON'T – and, frankly, if you have the right kind of help, there's no reason you should do it yourself – yes, you

---

[1] This is the first of many instances in the book where I've had to choose a pronoun to use. Because there's no unawkward, uniform way to handle this, you'll see I use "he" and "she" and "him" and "her" interchangeably and randomly throughout the text.

could clean your house yourself, cut your own lawn or hair or change your own oil in your car but many don't do that. Why? Because our time is not worth it and doing so detracts from our being able to do what we do best – or like the most. But, I'll be the first to acknowledge that finding the right help is not easy. Thus, I've included an Epilogue at the conclusion of this book that may assist the reader in that regard. My hope is that, once you're done with this book, you'll not only be better able to choose the help you need but also then be a more active, involved participant in that help.

A key aspect of this book is the "uncommon" part of its title. While in a general sense all the topics here – investments, estate planning, insurance, etc. - are "common" in financial planning, I try to focus on them in ways that, while not secret or complicated, are uncommon (and sometimes controversial). **That's because the common thinking or conventional wisdom often is incomplete, improperly focused, shortsighted, biased and sometimes it's just more sexy or fashionable than actually correct!** But, like other uncommon things in this world – gold, genius, spiritual enlightenment – if you have it and take advantage of it, it's incredibly valuable.

A related word of warning – one of the primary reasons people are so ill-served in their financial lives is that they follow the crowd. The crowd not only might be headed off a cliff together, it also gets most of its information from individuals or publications whose job it is to entertain (I call them "financial entertainers" – they most assuredly are not financial advisors). They know nothing (or, at most, sound bites) about an individual's particular financial situation yet often pontificate very confidently about what the person should or shouldn't do. If I did that in my business, I'd be stripped of my licenses and certifications, if not imprisoned! Although I may assert some things here fairly stridently, I don't want to be confused with the entertainers. Thus, please be aware that MY goal is to enable you to identify issues, think about things differently, ask the right questions and simply be a more well-informed consumer – don't take any of the information here as the gospel truth until you've thought it through (preferably with some outside help) and assessed its applicability to your particular situation. And, in exchange for this caveat, I hope you'll cancel your subscription to mass market financial periodicals and turn the TV or radio off when the latest financial evangelist appears!

So, what's next? Take an hour or two to read this book and go speak with your existing advisor or use the Epilogue to help you find one. Commit to taking the time to put your financial world in order so that **it's as fully protected as can be and does the most possible for you throughout your life (and beyond), giving you increased confidence about your economic situation.** And, I'd love for you to check in and let me know how it's going – **jbiegel@strategiesforwealth.com**. Looking forward to your financial success!

A note about the numbers used in the examples in this book: they aren't true! Although they have been chosen and calculated carefully to help depict particular concepts in a general sense, they should not be relied upon as anything more than a representation of an idea.

Money Profile Quiz

You may wonder whether you need what's in this book. Here's a very simple "quiz" to help you determine that (hint: a few "no" answers to these items means you should keep reading!):

	Yes	No
1. I know what would happen if I or a family member <u>cause</u> an accident and are sued or are <u>in</u> an accident that's someone else's fault.	___	___
2. I understand the provisions of my auto and homeowners insurance and know they're as efficient as possible.	___	___
3. I know whether my benefits at work are the best choices available to me.	___	___
4. I know whether my health insurance will cover me if I have extraordinary medical bills.	___	___
5. If I get sick, I know how much replacement income I will have and that it will be sufficient.	___	___

6. If I or a family member get sick and need to be taken care of, I know how long our money will last. ___ ___

7. I know how I may be impacted if my parents or siblings get sick and need care for a long time. ___ ___

8. My spouse/partner and I have up-to-date estate plans. ___ ___

9. I've made sure all of our beneficiary designations are appropriate and up-to-date. ___ ___

10. All the parties to my will (executor, guardian, trustees) are familiar with the roles I've put them in. ___ ___

11. I know how my affairs (financial and health) will be taken care of if I can't make my own decisions. ___ ___

12. I understand the various types of life insurance and the pros and cons of each. ___ ___

13. I know how any minor children of mine will be taken care of and provided for if I die. ___ ___

14. When I die, I know that my family will be able to maintain its current standard of living, including staying in our home if they so choose.   ___   ___

15. I know I have sufficient liquidity to deal with an unexpected emergency.   ___   ___

16. I save money systematically and understand where my current rate of savings will lead me.   ___   ___

17. I have made plans for paying for the higher education of my children and know the pros and cons of those plans.   ___   ___

18. I have a comprehensive investment strategy that takes into account all of my and my spouse/partner's assets.   ___   ___

19. I know the impact on my savings, investments and retirement strategies if taxes or inflation spike up.   ___   ___

20. I am confident I understand my retirement income needs and how I will generate that income until I and my spouse/partner die.   ___   ___

21. I am organized financially – I know what I have, where it is and how it all interrelates (and so does my spouse/partner).   ___   ___

22. I know whether or not I'm going to be able to leave a legacy for my kids, church, schools, etc. ____ ____

23. I know the different types of people offering financial advice and how to determine who I want to work with. ____ ____

LAYING THE FOUNDATION: PROTECTING YOUR MONEY

Chapter 1. Money and Creditors

Perhaps the most basic of human emotions is the desire to keep what we have – it goes back to the days of mastodon meat and clubbing someone over the head if he tried to take it away from you. And it extends in modern times to holding onto a variety of material goods, our stuff, our money! Putting aside your brother-in-law who always is trying to get you to participate in his latest get-rich quick scheme (you know not to do that, right?), for most of us, "creditors" are how we refer to those trying to get our money. Examples are credit card issuers or mortgage, automobile or student loan lenders. I'd call those "voluntary" creditors because one voluntarily – although perhaps sometimes with not enough thought – gets involved with them. "Involuntary" creditors are people or entities who sue us to get our money and win. This Chapter is focused on the involuntary type.

Basic Liability Protection

While there are a variety of ways to protect one's money from involuntary creditors (often costly and complex – offshore arrangements, trusts, etc.), for the vast majority of folks the greatest and most efficient protection can be obtained through conventional liability insurance. Initially, this is the liability protection associated with your automobile insurance and your homeowner's insurance. But, **you cannot stop there** – most car or homeowner's insurance coverage is unlikely to cover you for more than $500,000 of liability. While that may sound like enough to cover the majority of liability situations you're likely to find yourself in, it's easy to envision any number of scenarios where that $500,000 will be a drop in the bucket.

For instance, picture that you or a family member run a stoplight in your car and hit a minivan full of young anesthesiology interns on their way to a convention (or wherever young interns go!). Unfortunately, one or all suffer significant injuries and aren't able to continue their promising careers. If we assume on the low-end that they'd each make $200,000 a year for the rest of their 30 year working lives, to compensate them for that lost income, assuming a 5% rate of return, they'd each need to have a pot of money of approximately $3.2 million (and that's not even taking into account medical costs, pain and suffering and other damages that'd likely be added in). This may be an unlikely scenario but it's hardly out of the question – nor are many others like it (and, let's make it worse by assuming that you aren't a particularly sympathetic defendant because you had a couple glasses of wine before the accident – anyway, you get the idea).

Additional Liability Protection

I assume I have your attention now. The good news is that much of the type of liability described above is easy to protect against, through what's referred to as "excess" or "umbrella" liability insurance. The way it works is that your basic car or homeowner's insurance covers the first layer of liability – for instance, the initial $500,000 – and the umbrella policy covers beyond that. Because even the insurance companies assume that liability above $500,000 is a fairly unlikely event, the cost of the umbrella policy is modest for the amount of coverage it can provide you against a catastrophic event. Typically, your car or homeowner's insurance carrier will be willing to write umbrella coverage for you, although most require you to have both your car and homeowner's insurance with them.

Another aspect of umbrella insurance is **under- or uninsured coverage,** which is more and more rare – but important to obtain if possible. Under that provision, if someone is negligent toward YOU (as opposed to you being the negligent one), and they have little or no liability insurance for you to recover against, your insurance will cover you. Most car insurance already has such a provision but, again, it's a limited amount and we can't ignore the potential that YOU might be one of those injured anesthesiologists we discussed above. It would be a sad day if you became unable to work for the rest of your life and there was no place to go for compensation.

Coverage gaps. It's important to make sure that the "underlying" liability limits on your cars, home, boat, etc. match up with the amounts required before the umbrella policy will pay. This is especially relevant if you're getting your umbrella coverage from a different carrier. For instance, if the umbrella policy kicks in at $500,000 of liability but you only have $300,000 of liability coverage on your car, the unpleasant result will be that you'll effectively have a $200,000 "deductible" before the umbrella insurer will pay. Also, keep in mind that the umbrella liability policy **will not cover you** for any liability incurred in a business or professional capacity (like malpractice, liability for service on a board of directors, etc.) so the relevant insurance in those circumstances is key too. Finally, if your business includes owning and renting out a couple rental properties, even beyond insurance it may be important to hold those properties through a Limited Liability Corporation to further shield you and your family. If you're in that situation, that's definitely something to discuss with a knowledgeable attorney.

How much coverage? How MUCH umbrella coverage to obtain may be dictated by the limits your insurer imposes – many won't provide more than $5 million. Throughout this book, I explain that the way I urge my clients to think about amounts of insurance coverage of a variety of sorts is not to try to engage in some abstract calculus about whether they "feel" like an extra $X of premium is worth an extra $Y of coverage – that's meaningless. What will be meaningful is to figure out how much coverage you'll want to have if/when the bad event happens – and I hope it's obvious that the answer is **you'll want as much coverage as you can get** (understanding that even that may not be enough if all those anesthesiologists sue you!).

You may find that the insurance company will try to help you determine the "right" amount of coverage by asking about the size of your assets to figure out what you stand to lose in a lawsuit if you don't have enough insurance. That's a fine starting point but an equally significant risk people face if they don't have enough insurance or assets to satisfy a creditor is that the creditor may try to **garnish some portion of the person's future income** – for as long as it takes to satisfy an otherwise unsatisfied judgment. For those in their prime earning years, that could be a worse result than losing some assets. Many insurance professionals and attorneys will tell you this is an unlikely scenario – I agree, but I sleep a lot better at night knowing I have a boatload of umbrella liability insurance in place for a relatively small cost.[2]

---

[2] The good news is that some assets aren't even accessible by creditors – 401(k) and other "qualified" retirement plan monies are statutorily protected in most cases; your primary residence may be safe; and life insurance asset values are protected to a greater or lesser extent in most states. That means that things like brokerage accounts or investment real estate may be exposed to creditors.

Again, there are other more complex and costly ways to protect your money. Indeed, those may be appropriate for you at some point but, **for now, you should obtain the maximum amount of umbrella liability insurance available to you.**

Insurance Efficiency

While we're on the topic of "property and casualty" insurance, another consideration is whether your coverage is as efficient as possible. Specifically, many clients I encounter have deductible amounts on their car and homeowners insurance that don't make sense (except for the insurance company). For instance, having a $250 deductible on your car insurance in the event of a collision costs a lot in premium in comparison to a $500 or $1,000 deductible. And, in practical reality, it doesn't take much of a fender-bender to have damage above $250.

Most people are unlikely to put in a claim for small amounts they could pay out of their own pocket because they know the likelihood is that the insurance company will raise their premiums as soon as they can to begin to recoup the loss. And, it's not correct to think about it in terms of "… a $500 deductible will save me $50 of premium a year over a $250 deductible so I'll 'win' if I make it for five years before I have an accident because then I've saved the difference between the $250 and $500 deductible." That's wrong because, in reality, you NEVER would have put in a claim based on the $250 deductible to begin with so anything you save with the higher deductible is a win. Your primary decision is to determine your threshold of "self-insurance" pain and then set your deductible (both for cars and your home) at that level. By the way, a nice byproduct of the increased deductible is likely that you'll have some freed-up premium dollars to pay for the umbrella liability insurance coverage you'll be getting.

Protecting Your Home

Although we've focused mostly on liability issues in this Chapter, another "big ticket" area to be sensitive to is the amount of property damage liability on your homeowner's insurance coverage (meaning how much the insurer will pay for damage from a fire or other causes). In the "olden" days, most homeowner's insurance policies had guaranteed replacement cost provisions – so that, even if you only had $200,000 of stated property damage insurance coverage on your house, if it cost $400,000 to rebuild it to its former condition (factoring in upgrades, new building codes, etc.) the insurance company would have to pay for that. Such coverage still is available (obviously at higher cost) but more and more policies limit coverage to the stated insured amount, sometimes plus a 10% or 25% margin for error.

The limited types of coverage are not "bad" but make sure you know what you have (often the limited policies have the word "guaranteed" in their description when that is not technically accurate). And, if it is some limited form of coverage, **it's important for the homeowner to be sure the property is insured for a satisfactory amount since the risk of underinsurance now is borne by them, not the insurer.** Although you don't need to insure the value of your property that's attributable to the land (and perhaps you can assume that, even if your house totally burns down, the foundation still will be usable), the rule of thumb used by some property and casualty insurance experts is to have property damage coverage in an amount of $300 times the usable square feet in the house. Thus, a 3,000 square foot house should have approximately $900,000 in property damage insurance coverage – obviously dependant to some extent on location and type of construction.

One last issue related to homeowner's insurance is that it is wise to have records of what's insured – preferably a video you take of the house and its contents and narrate as you go along (and then store copies of the video somewhere else). At the very least, this video will be a helpful memory "jog" if any loss occurs – and, at best, it may help you in any dispute about coverage with the insurer – e.g., "yes, we did have the custom crown moulding in the living room!"

One More Layer of Protection

Finally, there's another valuable creditor liability protection measure that is contrary to popular wisdom. Specifically, most married couples end up titling their cars in the names of both spouses. The usual (and correct as far as it goes) rationale for this is that the cars will seamlessly transfer to the surviving spouse at the death of the other. On the other hand, consider this scenario: one spouse has an at-fault accident, is sued for his negligence and the amount of insurance and assets in his name are insufficient to satisfy the injured party. In such an event, the plaintiff might well try to make the case that the other owner of the car (the other spouse) is jointly responsible for the first spouse's negligence. If that argument can be sustained, then the "innocent" spouse's assets (and income as we discussed above) are exposed, as well as the joint assets of the spouses (i.e., their house), which formerly were shielded if only one spouse was negligent. A scary scenario – perhaps unlikely - but one I tell my clients is not worth having to worry about just so that cars get transferred more easily if one spouse dies. As a result, the best strategy is to title cars individually in the name of the spouse who primarily drives each car. This is easy to do when you buy a new car. For existing cars, most states' Department of Motor Vehicles have a form whereby the spouses can jointly gift a car to the other spouse (usually for only a modest fee).

Uncommon Takeaways

- ▶ Maximize liability coverage and deductibles.
- ▶ Protect your house fully from damage (and document what you're protecting with video or at least pictures).
- ▶ No joint titling of cars.

LAYING THE FOUNDATION: PROTECTING YOUR MONEY

Chapter 2. Money and Sickness

I'm no psychologist but it is apparent that one of our natural human tendencies is to assume that current conditions (whether good or bad, but particularly good ones) will continue unchanged into the future. This assumption often is held by young and healthy folks who believe they'll always be young (or at least healthy!). My job, as much of a "downer" as it might be, is to urge people to plan for the usually inevitable bumps in the road. I try to get my clients to realize that there are **things they need to get right the first time** – for instance, there's no "do-over" if you cause a bad accident and don't have the requisite amount of liability insurance discussed in the prior Chapter – you can't get more after the accident! Similarly, that accident also may result in your no longer being able to work – or at least being out of work for an extended period of time. What's your plan in that case? This Chapter is about "pre-planning" (a terrible term but I think it helps get the point across) in a variety of ways relating to sickness (including disability) – whether yours or your loved ones.

Medical Costs

I wish I could be more helpful here – this is one of those areas where "it is what it is." Medical costs and the related insurance costs are likely to keep going up. Certainly, if your employer makes available health care flexible spending accounts (where you have money taken out of your paycheck pretax to use to pay for out-of-pocket medical costs during the year), you should take full advantage of that. Also, depending on your situation, you may be better off with a lower-premium, high deductible health plan option where you save and invest the dollars you would need to satisfy the high deductible in a health care savings account. Unlike the flexible spending account, these funds actually can be invested and earn money and also do not have to be used or relinquished in each calendar year but can be rolled over indefinitely from year to year.

Finally, in terms of protecting one's money, keep an eye out in the medical plan choices you have for whether the insurer imposes a lifetime coverage limit. Increasingly, there are $1 million or $2 million caps per person on how much the insurer will pay. Unfortunately, the cost of a long hospitalization, accompanied by complicated, cutting-edge treatment, can exceed those limits. Thus, to the extent you have the choice, it's best to choose the medical plan that has "unlimited" in the "lifetime benefit" column.

Lost Income Due to Illness

For much of one's life, her most valuable asset is the ability to earn an income, so it's critical to protect that in the event you can't work for an extended period of time. Many employers will pay some or all of your income for a period of time (the traditional "sick leave" concept) but rarely for more than six months. A few states and federal Social Security provide payments if one is disabled but those amounts are both small and typically require substantial incapacitation before they kick in. For those in blue collar jobs, worker's compensation payments may provide coverage for on-the-job injuries. However, for the vast majority of people, traditional disability income insurance – either on a group (through an employer for instance) or individual basis - is critical.

Group Disability Insurance. Group disability insurance coverage may be tempting because it's either paid for in whole or in part by one's employer or otherwise is relatively low-cost. Unfortunately, the old aphorism that "you get what you pay for" definitely applies in this instance. If the employer pays for the coverage, then any disability insurance payments received will be taxable. Further, group coverage typically is limited in a variety of ways compared to individually-owned coverage. For instance, it may only pay for a limited period of time (typically 2 to 5 years) if you can't perform the job you were doing immediately prior to the disability; but if you then can perform any job, payments may stop. Further, if you return to work on even a part-time basis, payments may cease. And, the premiums are not locked in – generally they go up as you get older and, if you ever want to leave the employer and turn that policy into an individual policy, the premiums tend to get much higher (although, if you're sick at that time, it certainly could be worth continuing the coverage at almost any price). Nevertheless, group disability insurance is a lot better than no disability insurance so be sure you sign up for it – as much of it as you can get – if you don't have and can't get individual coverage in place.

Individual Disability Insurance. If you have the opportunity to pursue individual disability insurance, it's worth exploring with your advisor what's available to you. There are a myriad of variables in disability insurance but here are the key factors to assess:

- ▶ What is the maximum benefit amount? It's typically 60-70% of your income (on the assumption that the benefit you receive will not be taxable because you're paying the premium with after-tax dollars so 60-70% roughly makes you "whole"). Do not try to get creative and figure out how much less money you'll spend if you're disabled in order to justify reducing the amount of coverage you obtain. Yes, you might spend less on "business casual" clothes but I assure you that you'll spend more on other things you never envisioned! For those with higher incomes (or where a large portion of one's income is attributable to a bonus), you may need to pursue both a base policy and a supplemental policy to get sufficient coverage in place.

▶ How long will the benefit be paid? Most typical is until age 65 (with the idea that you'd have stopped working at that point anyway...). Again, don't undermine your protection by choosing coverage that lasts only for a few years on the assumption that your disability will be short-lived!

▶ How is "disability" defined? Ideally, it's that you are unable to perform the duties of the specific job you were doing immediately preceding the disability. The best policies are written that way; lesser-quality policies specify that, after a period of time, if you can perform other work, the disability payments may cease (for instance, a surgeon who no longer can perform surgery but can teach).

▶ When does the benefit first get paid? That is, what is the "elimination period" during which you have to be disabled (90, 180 days, etc.) before the policy will pay? If you have short-term sick leave at work or other assets to get you through the elimination period, a longer elimination period can help save on premium.

▶ Can the disability benefit be increased in the future without additional medical underwriting? If your income is likely to go up over time, this can be a valuable benefit as your spending rises to reflect your increased income but your health may not.

- ▶ <u>Is there a provision for a reasonable cost of living increase in the disability benefit while you're disabled?</u> You wouldn't want a long period of disability to cause the value of your insurance to be eaten away by inflation.

- ▶ <u>Is the premium guaranteed not to increase during the life of the policy and is it waived once you're disabled?</u> Both these provisions are critical and are characteristics of the best policies.

Care During a Long-term Illness

The sobering reality is that almost everyone will experience some period of incapacitating illness before their death. While the pure medical costs may be covered by health insurance/Medicare, what about non-critical care (of the type found with visiting nurses, assisted living facilities or nursing homes)? That is paid for by Medicare on only a very limited basis and then paid by Medicaid for low-income, low-asset individuals. Unfortunately, the vast majority of disability insurance terminates at age 65 so it's important to focus on how you'll handle yours (or a loved one's) extended illness (and, even prior to age 65, it's unlikely that disability insurance will be sufficient to fully pay the costs of custodial or nursing care).

Those with substantial assets may be able to fund a long stint of care out of pocket. But, in any event, please don't underestimate the cost – as of this writing, the average annual cost of care in a facility like a nursing home is over $70,000, and much higher on the East and West coasts. If one needs significant nursing care at home, the cost can be over $100,000 a year.[3] Thus, even those with significant wealth may consider using long-term care insurance as a way to shift the risk of a long-term illness to an insurer – thereby preserving a legacy for their heirs, charities, etc. For those of lesser means, counting on governmental programs like Medicaid or the kindness of relatives for care is an iffy proposition. In such cases, long-term care insurance can play a compelling role. In general, it begins to pay (after any "elimination period", discussed below) when one is unable to perform at least two of six "activities of daily living"[4] or has a "cognitive impairment" (such as Alzheimer's disease). As with disability insurance, there are many "bells and whistles" associated with long-term care insurance but here are a few key considerations:

> ▶ Financial strength of the insurer: This is a long-term undertaking so you want to be sure the insurer will be there if and when the coverage actually is needed. Further, because the premiums for long-term care insurance are not guaranteed not to increase (and, indeed, there recently have been some notable increases), you want an insurer that has prudently priced its policies and may be better able to stand behind the pricing of the coverage it's offering.

> ▶ Joint spousal coverage: Insurers often will offer substantial discounts or desirable joint coverage provisions if both spouses obtain coverage at the same time.

> ▶ Amount of coverage: Long-term care insurance coverage typically is expressed in terms of a "daily

---

[3] U.S. Department of Health and Human Services, National Clearinghouse for Long-Term Care Information.
[4] "Activities of daily living" under long-term care insurance policies usually are: bathing, continence, dressing, transferring, toileting and feeding.

benefit" – that is, the cap on how much the insurer will pay for each day of care. The "right" amount is a function of what other assets and income you might have to pay for care, how much of that you want to preserve for your heirs, in what area of the country you might anticipate receiving care, and other factors that should be discussed with a professional advisor.

► Cost of living adjustments: With the increasing cost of health care, it's almost a certainty that the initial daily benefit you choose will become less and less sufficient. High-quality policies will build in an annual adjustment (3% or 5% typically) to the daily benefit amount. Other policies simply offer an option to elect an increased benefit amount each year for a to-be-determined higher premium each time there's an increase. It's generally better to pay for the cost of living adjustment to be embedded into your policy; otherwise when the opportunities arise to increase your coverage and you have to pay more premium, there's the potential you'll pass on it, which will cause the effective amount of your coverage to be reduced over time.

► Facility vs. at-home coverage: Some less expensive policies (particularly group-sponsored ones) limit or exclude payment for care in one's home. For most people, being cared for at home is their first preference so don't overlook this feature. In addition, high-quality policies can include a feature where it's possible to use the policy benefits at least to some extent to compensate a caregiver who is a family-member.

► Elimination period: This is the period of time during which you have to be in the condition necessary to receive long-term care benefits before the benefits actually begin. The longer the period, the lower the premium. Be careful, however, you don't find yourself in a position where you're unable to take care of your needs during the elimination period.

▶ <u>Length of coverage:</u> Some data indicate that the average stay in a nursing home is approximately three years so you'll often get advice that obtaining long-term care insurance providing coverage for three years (which reduces the premium cost) is sufficient. Personally, I think this is not a good average to rely on – number one, is it really reliable? Might it be skewed by the fact that most people resist going into a long-term care facility for as long as possible and indeed needed care (perhaps at home) for a much longer period of time? And number two, even if it's not skewed, I don't want my clients to take the chance that they're not the average (one of my grandparents was in a nursing home for <u>fifteen years!</u>).

As of this writing, there are many uncertainties in the long-term care insurance market – some carriers are seeking to substantially increase premiums on new and existing policies, some are exiting the market altogether and there generally is a concern that the costs associated with offering this kind of coverage are not going to be sustainable. In addition, there is the fundamental problem that long-term care insurance is another one of those products that, if all goes well, you hope never to have to use – so the premiums are all money down the drain. Thus, it is important to consider whether there are other ways to bear the very real potential costs of long-term care. While having lots of money could be a solution, there are other insurance products (such as annuities and life insurance) that may have provisions that enable them to be used as a supplement to (or possibly in lieu of) long-term care insurance. These may provide for benefits to be used for long-term care on similar terms as long-term care insurance but also maintain the flexibility to use the benefits for other purposes if long-term care is not needed.

Loved Ones and Long-Term Care

Finally, I sometimes find clients are simply too young to qualify for long-term care insurance (most insurers won't cover those under the age of 40) or are just at an age where they are more concerned with other aspects of their financial situation so long-term care issues are not top-of-mind. If you've read this book closely you know that's not a legitimate excuse under the "what coverage do you want to have after the bad thing happens" rule of thumb. However, putting that aside for now, if you're so young that it's difficult to focus on yourself and long-term care, a critical consideration is <u>others</u> – siblings, aunts, uncles and particularly parents – who might be in an objectively more urgent situation to need to be thinking about long-term care (and whose care needs could impact <u>you</u>).

In the case of one's parents, too often the lives of children are disrupted, if not derailed, by the long-term illness of a parent, because the children have to quit jobs, be away from their families, move, etc. Of course, a child should want to do whatever he can to take care of ill parents (or at least that's what I keep telling my kids!) but wouldn't it be better if the kids had gotten their parents to do some planning for the supposedly unexpected by acquiring at least some long-term care insurance (which the kids could fund if necessary)? And, if the parents are in a situation where they own or mostly own their home outright, one strategy worth analyzing may be to obtain a reverse mortgage on their house and use the proceeds to purchase long-term care insurance.

One last comment - not to be sexist, but the fact is that it's **women who are most impacted by long-term care considerations**. This is because (1) statistically, it's more often women who end up with the responsibility to care for parents and (2) women are likely to face the reality of taking care of themselves if actuarial projections come true and they survive their spouse. Thus, the woman may need to be the catalyst to get decisions made and, if resources are limited, it may be better to focus on obtaining long-term care insurance for her.

Documents You Need When Sick

Financial Power of Attorney. I find that, while many people understand they need to have a will in place, they have not given thought to the handling of their affairs if, as is often the case, they're incapacitated prior to their death. In that regard, having powers of attorney in place for others to make financial and health care decisions is crucial if you are unable to make your own decisions. Typically, these are done as two separate documents given the very different roles played by the person holding the powers of attorney. You want someone who can access your various accounts, pay your debts and so on – that's what a financial power of attorney is for and it's typically written as what's called a "durable" power of attorney so that it's not just usable if you're out of the country and papers need to be signed but also if you are in a coma or otherwise unable to direct your affairs.

Health Care Power of Attorney. This document gives someone else the authority to receive information about your medical condition and make decisions about your treatment. Note that the enactment in 1996 of the Health Insurance Portability and Accountability Act (what's commonly referred to as "HIPAA") among other things imposed stiff penalties on medical professionals who disclose your medical information to others - even a spouse - without specifically-worded authority. Thus, if you have a health care power of attorney written before 1996, it likely needs updating to include such authority.

<u>Medical Directive.</u> The health care power of attorney gives someone the authority to make medical decisions for you but a "medical directive," or what is sometimes called a "living will," can give that person your guidance about what steps you'd like them to take or not take when you're approaching "the end." What you choose – from being kept alive at all costs to no heroic measures being taken at all – is of course a completely personal choice. I simply advise people to consider addressing these issues if they have a strong feeling one way or the other. If your choice is to die naturally with no heroic measures, most people still want to be sure that any pain they have is relieved. Surprisingly, many living wills are silent on that point so make sure yours isn't! Finally, if you do create a living will, get it in the hands of the person who has your health care power of attorney and, ideally, in your primary doctor's files as well.

There's another consideration to keep in mind that sometimes gets lost in the legalities of all this: the medical directive is NOT the same as a "DNR" (for "Do Not Resuscitate") order. Indeed, it may be difficult to operationalize one's wishes in a medical directive if one already has been hooked up to a myriad of machines by the paramedics or hospital in the heat of the moment. Thus, if your status is such that a DNR situation is possible – that is, you have what's referred to as a "life-limiting illness" – make sure your wishes are well-known. That can be done in most states by using a state-approved DNR form that is signed by your physician. One's DNR order should be posted prominently (like on the refrigerator) to alert first responders.

Uncommon Takeaways

- ▶ Look out for lifetime medical insurance coverage limits.

- ▶ <u>Fully</u> and effectively protect your most valuable asset – your ability to earn an income.

- ▶ <u>Fully</u> protect yourself and your loved ones in the event of extended illness/incapacity and don't necessarily assume long-term care insurance is the most efficient alternative.

- ▶ Put Powers of Attorney in place <u>now.</u>

- ▶ Make sure your end-of-life wishes are clearly- and well-known (and that pain relief isn't unintentionally overlooked).

LAYING THE FOUNDATION: PROTECTING YOUR MONEY

Chapter 3. Money and Death

I know, you're saying to yourself "first getting sued, then getting sick, and now dying – how depressing!" I don't disagree but it's a lot more depressing, if not alarming, to be caught unaware. What all these scenarios have in common is that there's generally no predicting if or (at least in the case of death) when they'll happen and it's too late to address them once they do. **Thus, you want to be strongly positioned to deal with them as smoothly and as economically efficiently as possible.** Of course, death is the last thing most people want to think of but it's nevertheless a certainty that must be planned for.

Wills

Why have one? **As a general matter, if you have any assets to speak of, and definitely if you have children, you need a will.** Although each state has what are referred to as "intestacy" laws governing how one's assets are transferred after death in the absence of a will, you may not necessarily agree with the state's approach (for instance, if you're estranged from one of your parents and you don't want that parent to get any of your money, you need a will). If you have children, you'll want to use your will as the vehicle to designate a legal guardian if both of the child's parents are deceased. Otherwise, you open up the potential for an unnecessarily messy and ongoing process to have the courts designate and oversee a guardian. Similarly, you do not want children to receive any money outright from your estate. Technically, a minor cannot directly hold funds so, again, there must be some legal process in order to choose and oversee someone to hold and manage assets on behalf of children until they're 18, or possibly 21. Another problem is that there are few 18 or 21 year olds who can be entrusted with any meaningful amounts of money. Thus, you'll at least want to have a trust that comes into existence at your death to hold money for the children. That trust would have a trustee to decide how the money gets used for the kids' benefit until they reach some age or ages that you specify (based on your hope that they'll then be responsible enough not to blow the money all at once).

<u>Beneficiaries.</u> It's important to note that a sizable portion of most inheritances is from retirement accounts, pension plans, annuities and life insurance. The funds from all of these pass by contractual beneficiary designation so **it's critical to make sure those beneficiary designations match up with your intent under your will** (and, again, you would not want children to be named directly as beneficiaries of any of these). Further, your "estate" should never be the beneficiary of retirement accounts or life insurance for a variety of reasons, but here's just one example: if you set up your life insurance so that your spouse is the primary beneficiary and your estate the contingent, or secondary, beneficiary and you and your spouse die in a car accident that was your fault, the insurance proceeds conveniently flow to your estate as secondary beneficiary and, voila, are accessible to your creditors – such as the other people you hurt in that accident. That should not be the case if another person or trust is the contingent beneficiary.

One other technical issue that often is overlooked relating to beneficiary designations is that there will be costs (taxes, fees, etc.) to be paid in the final administration of your estate. Those have to come out of your estate's assets. If, however, so much of what you pass on passes outside your estate via beneficiary designations, then the actual value <u>in</u> the estate (and those who receive it) may be disproportionately affected by these costs. It may not matter if the inheritors/beneficiaries are all the same but, if not, this can sometimes be a major sticking point in what could otherwise be a smooth transition at death. This can be addressed by proper drafting of one's estate plan.

Those are the basics – but just as this book is not intended to be a self-service financial planning tool, neither is it intended to do that for estate planning. Thus, you need a professional to look at your particular situation. For those who will have significant assets at death, the strategies for protecting their assets need to go further.

Estate Tax Planning for Larger Estates (Up to $10 million for married couples)

Although the trusts referred to above are important for preservation and management of funds for younger children, they also can be used to accomplish other goals, particularly in relation to estate taxes. While the laws surrounding estate taxes are in a constant state of flux, such that it's difficult to characterize who needs to do more than basic wills and trusts, I'll try to point to some general considerations that should be addressed.

Use of Trusts. Under current Federal law one spouse can transfer an unlimited amount of assets to a U.S. citizen spouse free from estate tax and any person can transfer an amount equivalent to $5,000,000 of assets to any other person (again, U.S. citizens) without estate tax (some states exempt similar amounts from their estate taxes but many are lower). Further, an individual's $5 million exemption is "portable" and usable by their spouse in addition to their own $5 million exemption. Because this particular law is temporary, subject to some tricky technical limitations and there are other tax and non-tax reasons why it may not be wise for all of one spouse's assets automatically to pour into the estate of the surviving spouse, many trusts and estates attorneys structure estate planning such that the first-to-die spouse's estate passes in full to the surviving spouse but that spouse has the right to "disclaim" (meaning to give up or relinquish) some or all of that amount. Any amount disclaimed would go into a trust set up under the deceased spouse's will.

In this way, depending on his or her needs, strategies and the then-current Federal and state estate tax laws, the surviving spouse has the option to not disclaim and keep all the money or to disclaim some or all of it to pass to the trust. If he or she does disclaim into the trust (and if the law has reverted back to what it used to be where there was no "portability" of an individual's estate tax exemption), the first-to-die spouse's estate tax exemption can be preserved at his or her death by having an equivalent amount of assets held in trust for the surviving spouse and children to use; it just does not fully become part of the surviving spouse's estate. Then, when the surviving spouse dies, he or she still has his or her OWN estate tax exemption, with the result that substantially more assets are able to be transferred without estate tax. This is referred to variously as a "bypass" trust (the money "bypasses" the surviving spouse's estate) or as a "credit shelter" trust (the money is "sheltered" under the estate tax "credit" that enables an amount – currently the $5 million - to pass without tax).

Two caveats to keep in mind about structures like this: one, the "disclaimer" process has some technical requirements that must be closely followed (e.g., the disclaiming spouse must disclaim promptly and cannot have benefitted from the assets disclaimed). Also, to be successful it may be important to have sufficient assets in a particular spouse's name at death. If, for instance, $8 million of assets are in the wife's name at her death and only $2 million are in the husband's name and the husband dies first, depending on the law at the time, he may not be able to take full advantage of his estate tax exemption. (I recognize there may be countervailing reasons to have more or less assets in one spouse's name than another's and those should be factored into the analysis.)

Super Trusts. Although the trusts described above are intended to have a limited life (that is, until the second spouse dies or until the children are a sufficient age to have the remaining principal distributed fully to them), that is not necessarily the ideal approach. Depending on state law, it is possible to set up trusts that have an unlimited life and, by keeping money in trust, shield it from creditors and divorces of the beneficiaries of the trusts forever. Further, by allowing assets to stay in and grow in the trust, it may be possible to avoid estate taxes for future generations (think, for instance, of an example where the trust buys a house for the beneficiaries so the money/assets always stay in the trust and it's just the beneficiaries who change over time). Further, with the right construction, it is possible to give the beneficiaries substantial control over certain (not all) aspects of the trust, including who manages the trust on their behalf.

Estate Tax Planning for Very Large Estates

When a married couple has an estate in excess of $10 million under current law, more sophisticated strategies may be warranted. Suffice it to say that, if you die with assets greater than the combined estate tax exemption amount, it is not possible to pass the full amount of your assets to heirs. However, there is much that can be done to maximize how much gets passed on.

Gifting. You actively can reduce the value of your estate by using the ability to make tax-free gifts to family members during your life (right now, each spouse can gift $13,000 a year to an unlimited number of persons, plus up to $5 million, which reduces the amount of their $5 million estate tax exemption mentioned above). A primary reason for making any of these sorts of gifts early is the time value of money. By taking an asset that's worth, say, $1 million today and gifting it outside your estate and having it grow outside your estate to $10 million by the time of your death, you've removed $9 million from your estate that otherwise might have been taxed.

As you might expect, there's a quid pro quo to this: for the asset to be considered by the IRS to be truly outside your estate, you have to give up sufficient control of it so the IRS considers it to no longer be "yours." This is an area of much complexity and subtlety but well-worth exploring with creative experts if you have or may have assets above the applicable estate tax exemptions. For small and medium-sized business owners in particular, there is much unique and valuable planning that can be done to minimize taxes, keep the business going after death and treat surviving family members, other owners of the business and employees well.

Charitable Giving. Charitable giving can have tax benefits that are as great, if not greater, than gifts to family. As a matter of public policy, Congress has established a system whereby estate assets above a certain amount are subject to a tax – either involuntarily, as in the estate tax, or voluntarily by virtue of gifts to charities that benefit society as estate taxes do and, as a result, can reduce estate tax that otherwise would be due. People typically find the voluntary route (and the legacy it creates) much more appealing than having money go into the black hole of government coffers. Charitable gifts, of course, also can be done on a "lifetime" basis. A benefit of lifetime giving is being able to currently use the related tax benefits and for the donor to be able to see and even participate in the results of her giving. There are a myriad of structures and issues associated with charitable giving that are beyond the scope of this book and require both a knowledgeable and strategic advisor as well as technical specialists.

The downside of the voluntary approach is that it may leave even less for heirs than the involuntary route. With appropriate planning earlier in life, however, this does not need to be the case. Just a simple example: if one has a large IRA account that will be subject to estate tax (in addition to income tax) at death, donating it to a charity can avoid the taxes (that all told can slash away 80% or more of the value of the IRA). If the deceased donor had put in place sufficient permanent life insurance (discussed in more detail in the next Chapter) on her life (and possibly used an ILIT as described below to make it NOT countable for estate tax purposes, which is not possible to do with an IRA) then the donor's heirs get these funds and it shouldn't particularly matter to them that they don't get the IRA (although what they might get is an honorary seat on the charity's board of trustees).

<u>Irrevocable Trusts.</u> I mentioned above an "ILIT" (pronounce it correctly – "eye-lit" - and seem smart to your advisors) – it's an acronym for "Irrevocable Life Insurance Trust." As its name indicates, it is a trust that owns a life insurance policy for the future benefit of designated beneficiaries and, generally, cannot be undone or changed – thus, the "irrevocable" part. Actually, almost any asset can be conveyed to an irrevocable trust, not just life insurance, although life insurance is a common choice because it's relatively easy to handle. The idea of this irrevocable conveyance is that the life insurance asset then should not be part of the trust creator's (who's called the "grantor") estate for estate tax purposes and be protected from creditors. So far, so good. Indeed, at a later point in life when the estate tax potentiality looms most large, this may be a great strategy (although it's not something that successfully can be done in

contemplation of death so you have to live for at least three years after the transfer to effectively get the asset out of your estate for tax purposes). However, there are a number of countervailing considerations that should be addressed:

- ▶ <u>I urge clients to take the "irrevocable" part very seriously.</u> Although some adjustments potentially can be made after the fact, for all intents and purposes you should assume that the assets will pass to the beneficiaries (<u>e.g.</u>, children) you initially name in the trust document. And, if children (or their spouses) turn out to be problematic in the future, you may have made a costly decision. Further, given the ever-changing nature of the estate tax (and strategies related to it), you should be very sure that, unless you engage in this transaction, you're going to have an estate tax issue. Simply put, the burdens associated with this structure may not be worth the benefits to someone who is far away from the expected time of death.

- ▶ <u>The grantor of the asset to the trust is extremely limited in the benefits he or she can derive from the asset in the trust.</u> Thus, in the case of an asset like life insurance that may have been meant to serve "double duty" for its death benefit as well as the living benefits it provides (as described later), putting it in an ILIT may truncate those benefits.

- ▶ <u>There are meaningful costs to create the trust (mostly legal expenses).</u> Those costs can end up having a significant lifetime impact on one's wealth due to the associated lost opportunity cost (as described in Chapter 5).

- ▶ <u>One can't just put an asset in a trust and forget about it.</u> There are ongoing trust administration requirements/tax returns, etc. If payments to the trust must continue to be made (for instance, so it can pay life insurance premiums), there are some fairly complex procedures that must be adhered to in order to properly get cash into the trust.

▶ There may be unintended consequences of putting life insurance in a trust. For instance, it may inefficiently use up the gift tax exemptions available to the grantor. It may be preferable to leave life insurance in one's estate but still create an irrevocable trust and fund it with assets other than life insurance – perhaps an asset that doesn't require ongoing payments (which use up annual gift tax exemption amounts) but is expected to experience rapid appreciation. That asset then grows in the trust and, if properly structured, any income taxes due can be paid by the grantor without using any gift tax exemption (thus reducing the grantor's estate further and increasing the benefit for the beneficiaries of the trust because they'll end up with an asset whose tax basis is higher as a result). At some point in the future, the trust can use its assets to acquire the life insurance from the grantor of the trust. The cost to acquire a permanent life insurance policy roughly will be its current cash value, which often will be substantially less than the total death benefit of the policy. Thus, just as an example: if it took $1,000,000 of the trust's assets to buy a life insurance policy with a $3,000,000 death benefit and the grantor's (insured's) death is expected to be in the near future, this transaction has shifted much more assets out of the grantor's estate than if the life insurance policy had been put in the trust on day one (although there are some complex tax issues that must be addressed in a transaction such as this).

Estate Planning Potpourri

A couple other uncommon estate planning issues to consider:

Living Trusts. Some trusts and estates attorneys automatically recommend setting up a "living trust" (also known as an "inter vivos trust" or a "revocable trust"). Similar to an ILIT, this is a trust that's not created under a will but is created during one's lifetime and owns some or all of one's assets. Unlike the ILIT, however, it can be undone and, thus, there is no tax benefit to it. The most common reason for recommending it is that assets transferred at death that are in a living trust avoid the probate process and the cost, time and potential public disclosure associated with that process. Although in the past the time and expense of the probate process were important considerations, that generally no longer is true (however, in some states the process still is costly and takes a lot of time). **In the vast majority of states the benefit of a living trust is not sufficiently meaningful to warrant the additional cost and effort of the drafting and ongoing administration of it.**[5] (A noteworthy exception might be if one has assets – like real estate – situated in more than one state where having to go through multiple probate processes could be painful.) Any suggestion by an estate planning attorney that a living trust is necessary should be countered by a request for a discussion of the practical pros and cons. Further, keep in mind that often much of a person's estate (jointly owned accounts, certain real estate, life insurance or retirement accounts), if handled correctly, is not subject to the probate process/cost anyway!

"Second-to-die" Life Insurance. For large estates where there may be unavoidable estate tax due, along with some question whether sufficient liquidity will exist in the right timeframe to

---

[5] For instance, for a living trust to be of any value, there must be assets in it; conveying assets to and holding assets in a living trust entails some complexity.

pay those taxes or other obligations of the estate, life insurance often is a solution suggested by experts. Invariably, however, the life insurance they suggest is what's called "second-to-die" or "survivorship" life insurance. That is essentially one policy that covers both spouses but only pays out when the second of the spouses to die departs – the idea being that, due to the unlimited marital estate tax exemption referred to above, no tax will need to be paid until the second spouse's death. The rationale is that this product is nicely calibrated to come into play just when needed and, because the actuarial risk of this kind of life insurance policy is more appealing to the life insurance company, the premium is "cheaper." **What most estate and other planners fail to factor in is the true cost of this strategy compared to other alternatives.**

An estate planning attorney or life insurance agent's suggestion of a second-to-die policy should be followed by a request for a discussion of the pros and cons. In particular, there should be an analysis of the cost of the second-to-die policy relative to a normal "first-to-die" policy on the older spouse, which may entail a greater premium outlay but will cause wealth to flow in at the first death that can grow/be used by the surviving spouse (potentially for a long time depending on life expectancy differences between spouses) in ways not possible with the second-to-die policy. The point is that the second-to-die policy only does ONE thing and it does it in a rather inefficient way economically unless both spouses happen to die soon after it is implemented. There may be other alternatives worth considering that work better both in economic terms and otherwise.

Where the Rubber Hits the Road

One last bit of practical advice – all the above deals with important legal documents and structures. But let's face it – the critical issues after one dies are things like – where are the keys to her car? Where is her will? Where did she have a bank account that we can use to pay the mortgage this month? and on and on. (And, I might add, if you have particular wishes about what should happen after your death – e.g., burial vs. cremation – while those often are expressed in wills, the will is usually reviewed too long after the fact to be much help so make sure those who'll be tending to you after death know your wishes.)

Without neglecting the legalities, I urge all my clients (no matter what their age or health) to "put their affairs in order" **TODAY** as much as reasonably possible. This means documenting where things are located, how to access them, who to notify, and so on. Knowing that those left behind will be free from needless turmoil and confusion will provide both you and your family with great mental tranquility, which is hard to put a price on.

Uncommon Takeaways

- ▶ Having an individually-tailored will is critical – as is making sure you've thought through how money flows at your death via beneficiary designations.

- ▶ Trusts are good; perpetual trusts are even better.

- ▶ But think twice about living trusts and irrevocable trusts.

- ▶ Gifts are good!

- ▶ Scrutinize the implications of "second to die" life insurance strategies.

- ▶ Guide those left behind after you're gone by providing a roadmap to your financial affairs. Ideally, have a practice "fire drill" of how things will play out at your death.

LAYING THE FOUNDATION: PROTECTING YOUR MONEY

Chapter 4. Money and Life (Insurance, that is)

On one level, life insurance is easy – you get a policy, you die, the life insurance company pays your beneficiary. But, that's just the tip of the iceberg – how to determine what amount of life insurance to have, of what type or types, what company to use and how to manage it on an ongoing basis all make a seemingly straightforward decision more complex so I'll break it down a little here.

Life Insurance and the Right Amount

At its core, life insurance is intended as a replacement for lost human capital – the ability of someone to produce an income or otherwise provide value. So, just as you want insurance to replace your house or car if they're destroyed, life insurance is necessary to replace lost human capital when one dies.

Needless to say, no amount of money can replace a loved one. However, from a more analytical standpoint, the "right" amount is the amount that represents the most you can be insured for. What is that? Life insurers will not (despite what you've seen in the movies) insure you for more than you're worth – that theoretically would create what's called a "moral hazard risk" whereby your loving beneficiary might decide to loosen the brake lines on your car because you're worth more dead than alive! The most you actually can be insured for is what the life insurance industry calls your "human life" or "economic life" value. That is, if you were to die tomorrow, what pot of life insurance proceeds would your beneficiaries need in order to replace your economic value to them? There are a myriad of complex mathematical contortions that some go through to arrive at this number but there is a much simpler and effective approach, which also happens to be the way the life insurance industry calculates how much insurance they'll let you have. Here's an example of how it works:

> If you're in your prime earning years (say age 30 to 50), and you're currently making $200,000 a year, what pot of money would your beneficiaries have to have to replace you economically (that is, replace the $200,000 you're bringing in)? The insurers assume that that pot of money would have to be invested fairly conservatively in order to preserve it for a long time if you died tomorrow and they typically use a "conservative" rate of return of 5% (which may be pushing it these days!). So, that's easy math: if your beneficiaries had a pot of $4,000,000, that would yield $200,000 annually if invested at 5%. That $4 million is probably the most life insurance you can get today in the aggregate from any number of insurers, even though it takes no account of the impact of inflation, other increasing costs of living and that you'll likely be earning more and more over time. So, it's not ideal – I might even call it the bare minimum - but it's the best you can do.

Getting by on less. People sometimes mentally start to chip away at the amount attributable to their economic life value by thinking there will be one less mouth to feed so that will save something; or maybe the surviving spouse could sell the house; or maybe go back to work; or maybe they could dip into that $4 million and not just live off the interest, etc., etc. All that is meaningless in real life because we're not trying to figure out how the family can survive or "get by" when you're gone. They're already going to be reeling from your departure; the least that can be done is make sure their economic world is not also devastated by having to sell the house, move, go back to work, etc. Truly, there is nothing sadder than the image of the widow coming back from the funeral and having to start paging through the employment want ads on the Internet. **Once again, just like you want insurance to replace your car or house if it's destroyed or your income if you get disabled, you want to fully replace the most precious thing you have.** The only legitimate hesitation I hear from people relates to the cost. Certainly, that's an issue but we'll discuss ways in this Chapter to make it NOT a cost to your financial world, but an <u>asset</u>.

What's so bad about dipping into the principal of the life insurance as justification for having less coverage? Once you start dipping into principal, you've opened the floodgates to a vicious cycle: you have to keep taking more and more to keep up the stream of income you want. If the market value of that principal declines, withdrawals will further accelerate the principal decline. In addition, dipping into principal may be necessary anyway in order to keep up with inflation over a long period of time and/or to reflect that the earning capacity of the deceased person increased since the life insurance was obtained but the life insurance coverage was not increased. Finally, some would say that the answer is your beneficiaries could buy an annuity with the life insurance proceeds in order to preserve the stream of income. That's fine (assuming they're OK with the downsides of annuities) but it's very unlikely to get them meaningfully more than that 5% stream of income we assumed above, even though it does deplete the principal base put in! Thus, don't cut it any closer than necessary – get your economic life value in coverage.

Life Insurance on Spouses

What about the economic life value of a spouse who earns little or nothing in the marketplace? Obviously, that spouse can have tremendous economic life value, just not calculable as simplistically as for someone with a steady salary. For that person, many insurance companies will consider approving life insurance of up to 50% of the amount the higher-earning spouse has. And rightly so too – to replace that spouse's contribution to the household, hiring someone to do what they do, after-tax, can be an expensive proposition. But, a less-understood consideration is: what impact does the "stay at home" spouse's departure have on the working spouse's ability to earn an income? For instance, if there are children at home who have just lost a parent, is the other parent really going to want to continue to operate on the 24/7 high-energy level he or she did before? Thus, **a major reason to have life insurance on a lesser-earning spouse is to protect the lost income of the higher-earning spouse** – who may want or need to ratchet down their income-earning ability.

Life Insurance on Children

Many people find the idea of life insurance on children abhorrent – they don't want to think about and they certainly don't want to "profit" from a child's death. That, however, is the least of the reasons to have life insurance on children. Assuming the parents have maximized the coverage on themselves (because, again, the death benefit to replace economic value in the event of "untimely" death is the primary motivation), having the right kind of permanent life insurance on children that can grow for many, many years and often can have provisions to increase the death benefit at various intervals over their lifetime no matter what their health, is a beautiful gift parents can give to their children. They will have begun a program of protection and asset growth that will serve them incredibly well for a long time to come.

Types of Life Insurance

Let's be clear at the outset about the fundamental point: **most people do not have enough life insurance in place today.** As with the other areas mentioned so far in this book that involve protecting you and your family, you need to fix that as soon as possible. This section will help you better understand how to get that done in the most economically efficient and powerful manner possible.

Temporary or "Term" Life Insurance

Temporary life insurance usually is called "term" insurance because it has a fixed premium for a term of time – generally from 1 year to 30 years, after which it ends – sometimes it can be renewed after the term expires, sometimes not. It's low-cost because, in actual dollar/cash flow terms, the premium is low. Why is that – are the insurance companies mispricing it? No, of course not. The reason is that their data show that, once they've approved someone for insurance, it's highly unlikely the person is going to die while the insurance is in force – either because they outlive the term of the insurance or because they drop the insurance early. This is borne out in the actual industry statistics – the vast majority of term life insurance never pays out a death claim!

With term insurance, the proposed insured is in the position of trying to figure out what the "right" term is – which, like most things involving predicting the future, is *really* hard to do. People are left to go through a rough calculus in their heads about when the kids might be done with college and/or when their other savings may have built up enough to supplant the need for a chunk of life insurance, etc. Unfortunately, the reality is that, when the end of the term – say it's 20 years – comes along, most people are not at all sanguine about the overnight disappearance of what they and their loved ones considered a real asset. It often turns out that the kids aren't done with college, or they're back home again, or the grandkids are living with them and/or there's been a market downturn and they don't have the big pot of money they thought they'd have, etc.

As a result, the insured's (and his heirs') loss is the insurance company's gain. Most term insurance premium dollars are retained by the insurance company because there's never any claim to pay. To the person paying the premium, this insurance means protection against the worst case scenario for some period of time, which is valuable. But, on the assumption that the insured <u>does</u> outlive its term, what is its <u>real</u> cost? To determine that, we need to consider not just the spent premium dollars but also the related *lost opportunity costs* – meaning the economic cost of the lost opportunity to invest money because it's been spent on something for which there's no return. If we assume that $1 million of 20 year level premium term insurance on a 35 year old has a premium of $1,000, that's a $20,000 cost over those twenty years. But the <u>true</u> economic cost is more properly calculated based on the lost opportunity to make money on that $20,000. If it could have earned 5% a year for those twenty years, that's a total cost of approximately $34,700. But the loss doesn't stop there. When the term of the insurance expires, the former insured is only 55 years old but that $34,700 is lost forever from his balance sheet. So, if we assume that that 55 year old lives another 40 years and could have continued to invest that $34,700 at 5%, the lost opportunity cost is more like $244,000! And, of course, that cost actually continues after the insured's death because his or her heirs don't inherit that pot of money.

The protection that term life insurance buys for your loved ones is incredibly important and it may well be the right thing to do in order to get the necessary protection in place. Unfortunately, however, the <u>temporary</u> nature of term insurance requires you to die at the "right" time to get actual value out of it. It's just like other kinds of insurance – car insurance, homeowner's insurance, disability insurance – in that the way you "win" the game is by not having used it. But, there's one key difference between life insurance and those other kinds of insurance: you WILL die some day so, if you have life insurance in place when you die, it will pay out. Thus, my preference for my clients is to save them the potentially hundreds of thousands of dollars of lost opportunity costs of term life insurance and instead get them the other type of life insurance, which is permanent. In that case, unless the policy owner cancels it early, the policy WILL be around at death and, barring extraordinary circumstances, WILL pay out more than the premium paid into the policy.

Permanent Life Insurance

All life insurance is fundamentally the same. Based on age, gender, health, lifestyle and the law of large numbers, the insurance company calculates how much premium it must collect on each insured to cover its costs and earn a profit. For those who are actuarially likely to die sooner (older people, sicker people, males) the insurance company has to charge a higher amount of money to cover its risk. Term insurance for most people is low-cost – because it just covers the time period when the risk to the insurance company is very low (if you want to see this concept in action, ask how much term insurance costs on a 70 year old). In the permanent life insurance world, the insurance company knows that it is theoretically on the hook for the insured's entire life and that, no doubt, the insured WILL die at some point. As a result, the insurer needs to figure out a way to get compensated on that policy for the increasing risk it's exposed to. It does that in different ways on different types of policies. To differentiate the key types of permanent life insurance in that context:

> Universal life insurance: Essentially, it is permanent term insurance – one can keep it for their entire life and it'll pay a death benefit whenever one dies but typically that's all – it usually has no other significant value. The insurer sets a minimum interest rate that is used to credit

earnings on the premium to pay the costs of the policy; that interest rate varies over time. If it is more than enough to cover costs, then the policy grows what's called a "cash value" or "surrender value", which is real money that can be withdrawn or borrowed against. If the interest rate is not high enough to keep up with the increasing costs of the insurance as the insured gets closer to death, the owner of the policy must add more money to the policy to keep it alive (no pun intended) or else let it lapse and walk away with whatever surrender value remains. Because the premium for universal life policies is typically set to the bare minimum to keep the policy going, there generally is no leftover surrender value on these policies. A more recent innovation is so-called "secondary guarantee" universal life insurance where for a higher, but fixed, premium the insurance company will guaranty that the initial amount of death benefit always will be in place so long as the premium continues to be paid.

Variable universal life insurance: Essentially the same as basic universal life insurance but it puts the investment responsibility on the owner of the policy, who directs the investment of the premiums paid into the policy to a variety of choices of investments (basically, mutual fund-like vehicles). If the investments do well enough, the policy not only can keep up with the increasing costs of the policy but also potentially grow a cash value. Conversely, if the investments do not do well enough, then the policy may lapse unless additional funds are paid into it.

Whole life insurance: The granddaddy (grandmommy?) of permanent life insurance. What differentiates it from other permanent life insurance products discussed above is that it comes with guarantees. There is a growing guaranteed cash value account, which serves as a sort of collateral for the life insurance company. The cash value protects the insurer as its mortality risk increases with age so it can offer a fixed <u>guaranteed premium</u> amount that will support a <u>guaranteed death benefit</u> amount. The cash value and death benefit guarantees may be supplemented by dividends from the earnings the insurance company makes on premium payments that it invests in its "general account" (typically, mostly bonds and bond-like instruments). (Those dividends, however, aren't guaranteed and are determined annually by the insurer.) The dividends that are paid can be used to buy more life insurance and to increase the growth of the cash value of the policy. Unlike other permanent life insurance policies, there's no risk that there will not be enough value in the policy to continue to support the base death benefit; similar to those other policies, however, there <u>is</u> the advantage that existing value in the policy and future dividends may be used to pay future premiums.

The various types of permanent life insurance policies do share certain basic characteristics: subject to some complex tax law requirements, the value in the policy can grow and be accessed without tax, the death benefit usually is not subject to income tax and, with proper planning, can avoid estate tax as well. Depending on the individual circumstance, any of the three types of permanent insurance can be appropriate. In my experience, whole life insurance often is the best fit so I'll focus on it a little further here. I'll be direct and tell you that there is a lot of negative publicity around whole life insurance – I almost wish they'd call it something else so that some of the mistaken ideas around it could be shaken off. Let's spend a little time looking at some of the common criticisms and misconceptions about whole life insurance because that should also help to explain some of its **uncommon** attributes. In no particular order:

▶ <u>It's a bad place to put money.</u> Compared to what? Whole life insurance readily can serve as the stable component in one's financial plan. A major part of what determines the growth of a whole life insurance policy is fixed-income instruments like bonds, because that's largely what the life insurance company is using to generate returns on the policy. Depending on one's age and health, it's reasonable to expect that the long-run internal rate of return on a whole life insurance policy will approximate 4-5% on an annualized basis. This growth, while not initially guaranteed beyond the base guarantees of the policy, does become guaranteed (or "locked in" would be another way to say it) as achieved, which removes the volatility associated with other typical "stable" assets. The ability to access those funds without tax makes that 4-5% much more valuable, depending on one's tax bracket. To that 4-5%, one needs to add the cost recovered by not having to buy term insurance and the lost opportunity costs associated with that. Finally, large corporations and banks use permanent life insurance by the boatload to shore up their balance sheets. **If it's such a bad place to put money, there must be a lot of company CFOs out there who've been duped into buying it!**

▶ It "costs" a lot. No doubt, the cash flow required is much more significant than that required for term insurance. It's "you get what you pay for" – with whole life insurance, you are getting life insurance protection for your lifetime and you are creating a multifaceted asset, as opposed to a likely "sunk cost" in the case of term insurance.

▶ I won't need life insurance for my "whole life." Maybe, maybe not – as discussed before, circumstances often end up such that people have miscalculated how long the need would remain (and even if it disappears, it can reappear in the form of estate tax issues). But, if you happen to end up not "needing" it, it's even more powerful because of the greater freedom you'll have to

Money and Life (Insurance, that is)   51

extract value from it for yourself, as described in Chapter 8, Money and Its Use.

▶ You should "buy term and invest the difference." The theory here is that one should buy supposedly cheap term insurance (although recall that term insurance that doesn't pay out is anything BUT cheap) and take the rest of the amount that would have been spent on whole life insurance and invest it in more traditional investments. What actually often happens in this instance is that people end up "buying term and spending the difference" because they have no disciplined way to save it.

Further, this strategy is akin to saying, if you were looking to buy a 50 foot sailboat, that instead you should "buy a rowboat and invest the difference." Except - you're not looking for a rowboat – even if it might "cost" less and float on the water. It's equally nonsensical in the life insurance realm. Term insurance does the job, on a temporary basis, of replacing human capital. Whole life insurance does that too but in a much more efficient and multifaceted manner – one could view it as a "Swiss Army knife" asset because of its many uses. I'd suggest the way to look at devoting savings dollars to whole life insurance versus other alternatives is to use the following features to compare the alternatives where you might invest the "difference":

> a. Will your "difference" investment generate potentially a 4-5% annualized rate of return with very low risk and have that return locked in as achieved? If you consider that policy values can be accessed without tax, for someone in a combined Federal and state tax bracket of 40% (perhaps wishful thinking that it won't be higher!), that's equivalent to about 7-8% that an asset subject to ordinary income tax would have

to make. (And, as mentioned above, this rate of return actually is higher if you factor in the term insurance costs that you save because you don't have to buy term insurance, which of course you have to do in the "invest the difference" scenario in case you die before the difference grows large enough, or you never save the difference or it experiences a market downturn.)

b. For those (likely most everyone) who are seeking to have a stable component of their overall financial plan, whole life insurance in an excellent alternative or supplement. The return is similar to other stable assets but better because, once achieved, is guaranteed not to go back down. Indeed, if market interest rates rise and the life insurance company is able to earn more on your premium dollars, that could be reflected in higher cash value growth, which is the converse of many other stable assets where values <u>decline</u> as interest rates rise. **And, let's not forget that this particular stable component of your assets also happens to buy you the life insurance you need anyway.**

c. If you go the "buy term" route, you're faced 20 years or so down the road with the usually unpleasant slap in the face when your valuable term insurance is about to expire, you can't get or don't want to pay for more and the "invest the difference" gambit hasn't turned out so well for you. On the other hand, if you go the whole life insurance route and happen to conclude after 20 years that you don't "need" life insurance any longer, then **you simply cash in the policy, pay tax on any gain and walk away with a nice return over the preceding 20 years.**

d. Will your "difference" investment do all the other things whole life insurance can do: (1) keep growing if you become disabled by virtue of the "waiver of premium" rider (an additional cost) whereby the insurer keeps paying the premium if you become disabled; (2) be "hidden" vis a vis creditors (depending on state law) and the college financial aid process; and (3) be readily accessible without tax if properly structured if you need money for some opportunity or emergency, such as paying for long-term care or college? And, in the case of college, think about what you've accomplished with the life insurance: you've created a pot of money that can be accessed to use to pay for college – if necessary and appropriate when the time comes – without income tax (if properly structured), which is the same as a Section 529 college savings plan (discussed later). In addition, the life insurance provides the cushion to complete the college funding process if you become disabled or die – the 529 plan does neither.

▶ <u>You shouldn't mix insurance and investments.</u> I'd agree with this one after a slight bit of rephrasing: "you shouldn't put your insurance at risk of market performance." So, while universal, and particularly variable universal, life insurance do this, whole life, because of its guarantees, does not. Certainly it's possible that the policy may not grow as quickly as anticipated but the cash value WILL grow and will not go back the other direction and your life insurance death benefit is always guaranteed to be there, no matter what happens with the insurance company's investment of your premium dollars. And don't underestimate that the management of the life insurance asset is carried out by a battalion of professional money managers working for a huge life insurance company – something you aren't likely to achieve on your own or even with a broker's help!

- <u>It has no flexibility – including that you have to pay the premiums for your "whole" life.</u> No doubt, for the first 2-3 years, the premiums paid into a whole life insurance policy are used in large part to fund the initial set up of the policy – which includes the insurer's administrative costs and, most importantly, reserves against the death of the insured. Thereafter, the cash value of the policy typically begins to grow year over year by at least (and then more than) the premium paid into the policy. As a result, for the first couple of years, the policyholder is paying for the lifetime insurance costs and, therefore, there is little to no flexibility to do anything other than pay the premiums. **Thus, it is important to understand that whole life insurance is meant to be a long-term undertaking and is not for you if you keep it in place only a few years.** After that period of time, there is more and more flexibility – flexibility to use past and ongoing dividends to pay some or all of the premium for some period of time and flexibility to borrow (or even outright withdraw) funds from the policy for opportunities, emergencies or fun. And, at some point in the policy's life (typically well before the insured's death) there usually is enough value in the policy and enough dividends generated by the policy to cover fully the ongoing premium payments.

- <u>You have to die to get any value out of it.</u> This is absolutely not true. However, you'll have to wait until Chapter 8 for more on this.

- ▶ <u>Insurance people "sell" whole life insurance because they make big commissions on it.</u> As a percentage of the premium, the commissions on term life insurance and whole life insurance are very similar and are highly regulated by state law. But this should be irrelevant. That is because, if you are working with the right person who has the expertise to help you fully understand all the merits of acquiring whole life insurance and you've decided it makes sense (based, by the way, on numbers that already reflect the impact of the insurer's cost of compensation, among other things), why would it matter to you how much that person is paid and don't you <u>expect</u> her to get compensated? Further, going back to the rowboat vs. sailboat analogy earlier in this Chapter, when you buy that expensive sailboat, you know the salesman is getting a larger commission than if he sold you the rowboat but is that a factor in whether or not you buy the sailboat? Of course not – you're buying the sailboat because that's what you want!

- ▶ <u>One is exposed to the default of the life insurance company.</u> This is a legitimate risk but can be substantially offset by aligning yourself with a company that has a long and uncheckered history. The way to address this is to stick with the major mutual life insurance companies in this country, which typically have been around for 150 years or more and thus have "seen it all" and tend to have financial ratings at the top of the scale. But, undeniably, there is always a risk – perhaps a risk that wouldn't exist if the money were in a federally insured savings account but a risk that exists in some way, shape or form with all other alternatives (including other "stable" assets discussed above for which whole life insurance can be viewed as a legitimate alternative). I believe there most assuredly will be worse problems in our society if insurers like the ones I described above have issues honoring their policy obligations.

I'll readily acknowledge that there is no one "ideal" asset; if there were, everyone would know about it and just buy it over the Internet and that would be that. But, in the realm of the ideal, those people appropriately situated should work with an advisor to thoughtfully consider the merits of whole life insurance.

Other Issues to Consider

Amount to devote to life insurance. Many clients ask me how they should go about deciding how much money to devote to this part of their financial world. Of course, it's a case by case analysis but a helpful rule of thumb I use is generally no more than 5% of one's income plus 5% of one's assets. This is because the premium on a whole life insurance policy is a static amount, but it actually "feels" smaller over time – inflation is your ally in this situation as your income increases and thus makes the life insurance premium a proportionately smaller part of your cash flow. Then, if one's assets are growing in a healthy way, siphoning 5% off each year to create the life insurance asset may have little or no net impact on that overall pot of assets. Beyond this "5 and 5" rule, based on the other discussions in this book, there may be opportunities to redirect funds to the life insurance premium by no longer prepaying a mortgage or maxing out the funding of a 401(k) – in order to reduce risk and create greater benefits.

Group life insurance – friend or foe? **Let me make this simple: if you're not healthy, group life insurance offered through your employer or an association to which you belong may be your best option. If you're healthy, group**

life insurance is your worst option. If you're relatively young, you may find that, today, the premiums associated with your group insurance are very low. What you should consider is that group insurance is typically a type of annual (or at best 5 year) term insurance so the price goes up regularly – and goes up dramatically when you become older. Many group life insurance policies contain "portability" provisions in that you can carve out your own individual policy if you leave your employer. At that point, however, you go from being part of a relatively healthy pool of your colleagues at work to part of the general population and your premiums will increase significantly. So, the message here is not to rely on group coverage if you can help it – it's fine if you want a little "cheap" extra coverage for awhile, but it definitely should not be the foundation of your life insurance protection.

Beneficiaries and settlement options. Remember the discussion in the Money and Death Chapter about not having children as beneficiaries: they can't and shouldn't receive this money directly until they are capable of handling it (having your estate or ex-spouse as beneficiaries can be problematic too). Also, every life insurance policy gives the beneficiary choices of a "settlement option" as the way the life insurance proceeds are paid – they can be paid in a lump sum, turned into an annuity stream of payments or held by the insurer as an interest-bearing deposit. It is this latter option you ought to select when you initially set up your life insurance, and be sure to specify that the beneficiary has the right to change it to any other settlement option. The reason is: assume the insured dies in a car accident that's the fault of the beneficiary and the beneficiary gets sued by someone else who also was harmed in the accident. It would not be a good idea for all the life insurance proceeds to flow into the beneficiary while they're getting sued so that the plaintiff can have more money to collect. Better to leave the funds with the life insurance company and, when the lawsuit is done, the beneficiary has full rights to change the settlement option and collect the funds in a lump sum. (While this is definitely not a foolproof strategy, it falls in the category of being worth a try!)

Type of insurer: mutual vs. shareholder owned. Companies in the life insurance industry are essentially divided into two categories – mutual companies that have no stock but are owned by their policyholders and stock companies that are owned by shareholders. When you think about it, if you're a policyholder, don't you want your company to be focused only on you and not have to also satisfy the appetite of stock market investors? Particularly if you are looking at a dividend-paying life insurance policy like a whole life policy, you want that from a well-rated mutual insurance company so all its dividends inure to your benefit and there's not some kind of divided loyalty between you and the shareholders.

Uncommon Takeaways

- ▶ Don't underestimate the amount of life insurance you should have in place.

- ▶ Don't underestimate the real economic cost of apparently "cheap" term life insurance; however, if term insurance is necessary to get the right amount of coverage in place, so be it!

- ▶ Take advantage of the opportunity to create a multifaceted asset out of your life insurance decision rather than a net drain on your lifetime wealth.

- ▶ Stay away from group life insurance if possible.

- ▶ The right life insurance decision needs to include the proper beneficiaries, settlement option and type of insurer.

BUILDING THE STRUCTURE: GROWING YOUR MONEY

Chapter 5. Money and Headwinds

This Chapter is important for reasons that are both obvious and subtle. While everyone knows it's desirable to avoid an expense like taxes where possible, less well-understood is the difference between affecting things like taxes that act as a sort of "headwind" against growing wealth vs. growing wealth by making more money. Humor me for a moment and think of yourself as a little money factory – let's say you have to work 100 hours to make $10,000 ($100/hour) and it costs you $2,000 in commuting, coffee and lunch to make that $10,000 so you net $8,000. Thus, all other things being equal, if you wanted to net $9,000, you'd have to find a way to work another 10 hours ($100 x 10 = $1,000). But, if you could, wouldn't it be preferable/less stressful to net $9,000 by just continuing to work the same 100 hours and cut your costs by $1,000 by changing how you commute, bringing your lunch, etc.? It's the same way with money: it's a lot harder/riskier to generate more money out of the blue than it is to try to impact a known cost – like taxes. I'm sorry to be trite, but I think a variation on an old expression is appropriate to get the point across here: "A penny saved is more than a penny earned!"

Let's look at a few "big ticket" examples of how money is eroded by headwinds over time – none of them will surprise you but the impact of them on your money may. As you read further, you'll see that inflation, taxes and spending are going to happen and that there may be ways to ameliorate their impact. However, their inevitability means that the items covered in the following Chapters regarding saving, growing and using money are of critical importance.

Inflation

We as human beings tend to have short memories – and historic consumer price inflation is a prime example. In recent years, inflation in the U.S. has been running at very low rates (1-3%). In 1980 it was about 13.5%! Currently there's a lot of doom and gloom about the specter of hyperinflation (except when there's doom and gloom about the possibility of deflation). But, even if we assume inflation continues at its long-run average of about 3%, its impact on purchasing power is both meaningful and insidious (in large part because it <u>compounds</u> over time – this is the evil twin of the miracle of compound interest you've probably heard of!). At 3% compound inflation, 20 years from now $100 will feel like $55 and 40 years from now it will feel like $31. Literally, the things that cost you $1 today – even assuming modest inflation – will cost you $2 or $3 in retirement!

Further, I'm sorry to say that the average, generic reported rates of inflation mentioned above are likely not YOUR rate of inflation. That's because your consumption and spending habits probably don't mirror those of the "typical" family used in government inflation calculations. In addition, even if you ARE the typical family, there are a myriad of "costs of living" that continue to grow that aren't even part of the inflation calculation. For instance, how about the technological gadgets we seem to need to buy and then replace every couple of years? Such types of costs of living didn't even exist 10 or 20 years ago and show no signs of abating in the future. And then there are all those things that seem to wear out faster and faster (as in, "they don't make 'em like they used to") that need to be replaced. Or even stuff we feel we need to replace that <u>isn't</u> worn out – I have plenty of perfectly usable neckties in my closet but I keep buying more "fashionable" ones! The cost to your lifetime wealth of new washers and dryers, cars, ties, (or whatever) can't be underestimated.

It's doubtful the trends described above are going to change in our lifetime. What does that mean? **It means we shouldn't fool ourselves by underestimating how much money it's going to take for us to live the very long lives most of us will live.** This puts further pressure on saving enough and taking some risk to grow one's money – money in a "safe" place that's earning little or nothing may be "safe" in that the principal won't be lost in the traditional sense but it WILL be lost in that it will "evaporate" over time from inflation. But, even more importantly, it points to the criticality of making sure the right strategies are in place so that, rather than taking on levels of risk most people can't tolerate, this erosion can be offset by enhancing the use of wealth – more on that in Chapter 8.

Taxes

Yes, I know, death and taxes: they're inevitable. Certainly some taxes are unavoidable – for instance, the taxes on the regular salary income one earns. But, there are ways that even unavoidable taxes can be mitigated. These include taking full advantage of available mortgage interest and charitable gift deductions (rather than prepaying a mortgage and running out of that deduction at perhaps the very time it's most needed or deferring charitable gifts until you're dead when others benefit from them but not you). Then there are other places where taxes can be avoided (municipal bonds, life insurance, real estate to a certain extent). Why is this all important? It's because the tax bite (and here I include Federal, state and local income taxes) is the single-biggest eroder of wealth that exists.

The tax erosion goes beyond the basic tax bite that's taken on each dollar. If your choice is to do something that generates taxes, the payment of those taxes removes wealth from your world forever. Thus, if you had $1,000 to invest, it earned $100 in interest and you had to pay $40 in taxes (either out of the $100 or, more likely, from somewhere else on your balance sheet because you would have reinvested the $100), the real cost of the tax is what the lifetime loss to your economic world would be from having had to pay that tax today (and, actually, it has an impact even beyond your lifetime because your heirs won't ever inherit that money). If that's another 50 years, and that $40 could have earned 5% each year during those 50 years, I'm sorry to say that that $40 in taxes actually cost you more like $459. Again, to some extent taxes are unavoidable but my point is that, when they CAN be avoided, that avoidance can be very powerful in terms of long-term wealth.

And, you probably don't need me to tell you that the tax picture is not getting any better – the implications at the Federal, state and local levels of reduced revenues, ever-increasing expenses and fewer and fewer places to source additional revenues mean that higher taxes are almost inevitable. That has one major implication – if you can pay tax today or avoid tax altogether, that will be increasingly prudent and powerful. Thus, that should lead one to question sacred cows like tax deferral, in the form of 401(k)s or IRAs, for example. Even without the specter of increased tax rates because of what the economy has been through of late, given the history of taxes over the years, it seems overly optimistic to assume that the current historically low tax rates will continue into the future. The chart on the next page depicts the highest marginal tax bracket in each of the years since the Federal income tax was enacted in 1913. The average of these rates is nearly 60%; much higher than the current 35% top rate.

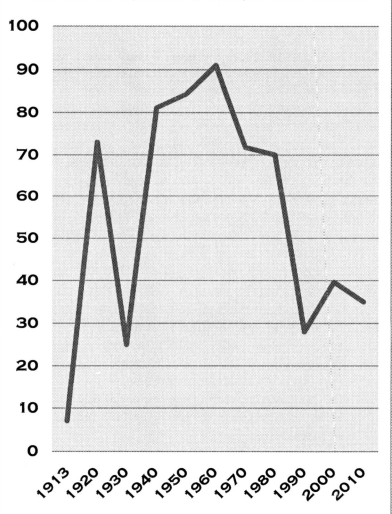

Given all this, might it be better to pay taxes on your income today and invest the resulting sum in tax-efficient vehicles rather than taking your chances that you'll be in a lower tax bracket when you retire and start taking money out of tax-deferred accounts?

Spending

Next, let's discuss the plain old issue of how much we spend day-to-day. I think life is too short to have to conform to a rigid budget and most people are mature enough not to be spendthrifts. However, what is important is that one be "present" to where their money is going. For instance, let's just take that daily Starbucks fix. Assume you spend just $3 a day only five days a week for your morning jolt, and you do that for 50 weeks a year. If you instead had been able to stomach the "free" coffee from the office coffee machine and could have invested the Starbucks money and made 5% over the course of a 30 year career, you would have had a pot of about $50,000. If we assume that at retirement you kick the Starbucks habit but still had that pot of $50,000 to continue growing at 5% during 20 years of retirement, it would have become $132,000. (For those of you who are more in the $10 a day, 365 days a year Starbucks realm, well, you can imagine how that math turns out.) I'm not trying to deprive you of this "treat"; I'm just trying to sensitize you to the impact this seemingly innocuous act has on your lifetime wealth. And, of course, the Starbucks example is replicated in other areas of one's life as well – going out to lunch, drinks, movie rentals, and so on.

The point of the example is that **all spending (as opposed to investing) has what I called a "lost opportunity cost" back in the discussion of term life insurance in Chapter 4.** Lost opportunity costs aren't inherently evil because the point of money is to be able to spend and enjoy it. Where there are ways to minimize the lost opportunity cost, however, the resulting ability to have MORE money to spend and enjoy can be powerful.

Debt

The topic of "debt" follows naturally from "spending" in that some (a lot?) of one's spending may be in the form of debt to buy a house, buy a car and to buy basically anything with your credit cards or otherwise "on credit." On the one hand, debt can be a beautiful thing if handled well – it can provide a tax benefit, it can free up funds to work elsewhere in one's financial world, and it can be a good strategy to let inflation play in your favor – if you can defer the repayment long enough into the future, you are paying back dollars you obtained on credit today with deflated dollars later on. Obviously, the other side of the coin with debt are the substantial headwinds it creates when, rather than you managing it, it manages you – i.e., you felt you HAD to buy something and you don't have the capacity to handle the related debt.

Clearly, there's an emotional aspect to debt that must be factored in as well: some people have an aversion to any kind of debt – that's not necessarily always the right economic decision but perhaps better to err on that end of the debt spectrum than on the other where debt is run up until bankruptcy is the only alternative. As with much of what's in this book (and life as well), a dose of moderation and balance in debt decisions can go a long way – if the debt is for a prudent purchase, its terms are manageable and you keep its existence on your financial radar screen, it can be a tolerable "headwind."

Uncommon Takeaways

▶ Don't underestimate the compound impact of inflation and taxes on your wealth.

- ▶ Don't get trapped into a "short-term gain for long-term pain" result by deferring taxes into a very uncertain tax future.

- ▶ Be <u>present</u> to how you're spending your money and using debt – neither is "wrong" if done with the right financial balance.

- ▶ Avoid expenses when you can, increase the efficiency of the expenses you can't or don't want to avoid, and make sure your overall financial strategy includes the ways and means to recover the costs to the greatest extent possible.

Building the Structure: Growing Your Money

Chapter 6. Money and Savings

This is a brief Chapter because it has a narrow focus: saving money for liquidity/emergencies. This is <u>after</u> the money you put into a checking account to spend on <u>basic, essential</u> day-to-day expenses and <u>before</u> the money you use to seek greater long-term growth, which we'll address in the next Chapter. Most fundamentally, before one does anything in terms of "investing" (including 401(k)s), <u>at least six months</u> of your total expenses (without scrimping) should be put somewhere where it can be readily accessed and, when accessed, can be relied upon not to be depressed in value. Typically, some portion of this always should be in the old-fashioned statement savings or money market account. Beyond that, other alternatives are:

- Short-term CDs
- Short-term, high-quality bond mutual funds
- Cash value of life insurance
- Untapped home equity lines of credit

Home Equity

The last item warrants a little more discussion. Theoretically, if you have a line of credit against your house that hasn't been used fully, you may have quick access to liquid funds because you probably even have a checkbook to use to access that line of credit. Recent experience, however, has shown that, the very time one might want to tap that line (because of some economic downturn), may be when the lender becomes concerned about you, your house collateral or just generally gets nervous and exercises its right to cut off future draws. **Thus, don't count too heavily on this as a source of liquidity.**

Prepaying a Mortgage

Many point to paying down one's mortgage (particularly by prepaying it) as a good savings strategy. They emphasize that it's equivalent to earning whatever the interest rate is on your mortgage (because you're saving the interest cost). It's definitely not as good as that – the determination of the real economic impact of the prepayment has to factor in three things: (1) the lost tax benefit from having less mortgage interest to deduct from your taxable income; (2) the long-term cost to one's wealth of having to pay higher taxes as a result and (3) the earnings that one might have been able to make on the funds instead of sending the money to the lender. The result of this calculation depends on its inputs but, in the majority of the analyses we run for our clients, the prepayment does not turn out to be the best <u>economic</u> choice (although for some people there may be a valid <u>emotional</u> reason to be debt-free).

The foregoing doesn't even factor in the main point of this Chapter – in terms of liquid savings, your house (although perhaps a safer place than others) is definitely not a <u>liquid</u> place to sock away money. Just like the home equity line of credit, the very time you'd need to access this savings (via a home equity loan, refinance or even sale) may well be the <u>worst</u> time to do so. I'm not averse to someone having the <u>ability</u> to pay down or pay off a mortgage if that turns out to be the right thing to do (for instance, because the tax benefits are reduced). But, wouldn't you be in a much stronger position if, instead of sending the money to the lender who isn't going to readily give it back to you, you had the money sitting somewhere (preferably growing too) where you can use it for whatever you wish – <u>including</u> paying down the mortgage if that's appropriate?

Ongoing Savings

Investments and Financial Planning

"I retire on Friday and I haven't saved a dime. Here's your chance to become a legend!"

Let's assume you have put a rainy day, liquidity fund in place. This can be a fairly static amount (obviously increased as your "cost of living" increases). Let's also assume you've taken care of the basic protection items referred to in Chapters 1 through 4 - the right amount of liability and disability insurance, that you've paid to get your will and powers of attorney in place and that you fundamentally have the right amount of life insurance in place if you get hit by a bus tomorrow. Now, going forward, your goal should be to save 15-20% of your after-tax household income. This is <u>not</u> money to be spent on your daily expenses OR the big-ticket items like the new phone, gadget, vacation, etc. I recommend you establish a separate account into which the money initially is deposited and that it's done on an automatic basis. Turn the page and we'll discuss what to do with the money that builds up in that account so that you don't experience the fate of the man in the cartoon above!

Uncommon Takeaways

- ▶ Do <u>nothing</u> (including contributing to your retirement plan) until you have your six-month liquidity fund in place.

- ▶ Make sure your liquidity fund actually <u>is</u> liquid!

- ▶ Be wary of using home equity as a source of liquidity or savings.

- ▶ Save 15-20% of your income on an automatic, ongoing basis.

BUILDING THE STRUCTURE: GROWING YOUR MONEY

Chapter 7. Money and Growth

Now that your financial world is protected as much as optimally possible, including having built up a liquidity reserve, we turn to making the most of ongoing savings. This Chapter focuses on money dedicated to long-term growth – for future use to pay for college, retirement, a second home, long-term care – things that are relatively (meaning 10 years or more) far out on the horizon.

My advice to clients in the realm of growing their wealth is first to **put aside focus on any one product and instead make sure they have an overarching strategy that guides their growth decisions.** Obviously, this is difficult given that everyone is exposed to narrow product sale pitches from people and institutions in the financial marketplace, including the mass media. And, even if a particular product actually is perfect for you, that conclusion should only follow the creation of a strategy into which it fits.

The Strategy

Risk Tolerance

The first and foremost consideration in investment strategy is risk – as in, "no risk, no reward;" "no pain, no gain," etc. And, on a long-term basis, that reward or gain is essential; otherwise one loses meaningful ground to the "headwinds" described in Chapter 5. The challenge is that, more than ever, people are fearful of risk because of recent economic turmoil. To a certain extent, that's healthy and constructive – because at times the opposite has happened and there was disproportionate enthusiasm (or maybe ignorance is a better word) about risk. On the other hand, if that fear leads to paralysis, that's not good. Indeed, I've had many people challenge my assertions about the merits of traditional "safety" factors like diversification and long-term investing by saying "but how about if it's *different* this time?" Of course, those people have in mind that the "difference" would be financial Armageddon. The only legitimate answer I have to that concern is that there is no investment strategy that will protect you if the world melts down; plus, who wants to live with that fear? And, in the more likely event the world continues NOT to melt down during our lifetime,[6] won't it feel worse to have stood by and fallen victim to known wealth-destroying monsters like the "headwinds" mentioned earlier?

Now that we've put the specter of apocalypse behind us, the right strategy starts with an honest assessment of your risk tolerance. I say "honest" because we're all cowboys and cowgirls during times of economic growth and "good news." Everyone feels they can tolerate volatility because they think of it in terms of "I might make 30% a year or only 5% a year; I can live with that" – when in reality what one may have to live with is losing 30% a year. The result if one really can't live with losing 30% a year is that they do dumb things – typically selling at the worst possible time and then sitting on the sidelines and missing opportunities, because they either can't or won't act quickly enough to take advantage of an upturn. Thus, it's important to work with your advisor to really assess your own brain, stomach, whatever, for volatility on the downside. That volatility typically is measured by "standard deviation", which is the

---

[6] Measured by the S&P 500 (large U.S. companies) stock index, the market has experienced multiple significant declines that all have been referred to as "different this time" but all of which have turned out not to have been "different!"

amount by which the performance of an asset or assets can vary (up or down) from its average performance. Then, it's still relevant to assess traditional risk tolerance factors such as when you'll need the money and for what but I believe those factors are a secondary part of one's risk tolerance. The result of this assessment then should drive the next factor: asset allocation.

Asset Allocation

Multiple studies[7] have shown that the single-biggest driver of long-term investment performance is asset allocation – at a high-level, that's the mix one has between equities (stocks), fixed-income (bonds and bond-like instruments) and cash. Below that level is having the appropriate mix of U.S. vs. international exposure, large company vs. small company exposure and then further subdivisions within those. Asset allocation has been determined to explain over 90% of portfolio performance over the long-term. Thus, it is important to work with an advisor to derive the right allocation for you. The idea of asset allocation is to create a scientific, unemotional approach to investing. It is not based on trying to pick stocks or bonds because of what you heard from your neighbor (or what the advisor heard from her research department). It also is not dependent on trying to "time" the market – knowing when to be in or out of certain investments (because to do that impossible task correctly you have to be right twice – once about when to get out and once about when to get back in – and most people who try it fail at both). The studies referred to above have shown that, even if one is the best of the best at stock/bond picking and timing the market, the impact on long-term performance far dwarfs that of asset allocation.

---

[7] An example is Brinson, Hood, Beebower, 1986. "Determinants of Portfolio Performance." *Financial Analysts Journal*, vol. 42, no. 4 (July/August).

Wide-Angle Allocation

Given the importance of asset allocation, it's obviously (although not so often done) critical that the allocation assessment be done across all the assets one has – those of both spouses, those in and out of retirement accounts, real estate, life insurance and so on. It would be unfortunate if your brokerage account has a well-thought out allocation but most of your money is in your 401(k) in a fixed-income fund because that's what you chose 10 years ago during new employee orientation!

Further, when possible, it can be beneficial to be strategic in allocating based on the tax treatment of different asset classes that make up the allocation. For instance, all other things being equal, those asset classes (like U.S. and international equities) that have the potential to be taxed at favorable capital gains rates and for which you'd like to be able to use losses to offset other gains should be in taxable accounts. Then, assets such as taxable bonds, which are taxed at ordinary income rates and (hopefully) have no losses that you'd want to offset against gains, should be held in tax-deferred accounts like 401(k)s or IRAs. Thus, you'll need to find an advisor who's willing to assist you in this approach – even though he actually may be handling only a piece of your overall investments.

Rebalancing

If establishing the appropriate asset allocation is so important, it stands to reason that it needs to be adhered to on a going-forward basis. As parts of that allocation go up or down in value disproportionately to other parts, it's critical to rebalance your holdings to get back to that original desired allocation. Because rebalancing can have transaction costs and tax implications, it's important to do so judiciously – your advisor can work with you in your particular situation to assess how often to do this – whether it's simply a calendar-based rebalancing or based on some percentage by which the allocation has to get out of balance, or some combination of both.

Implementation/Asset Location

You now know you need an overarching asset allocation strategy that matches your real risk tolerance but with what do you "fill up" that asset allocation? Or said another way, what's the "ideal" place to grow your money? The fundamental principle is not to put too many eggs in one basket (but you probably already knew that). Unfortunately, this is what many people do – whether it's too much money in their company's stock, their own business, in their 401(k), in college savings plans - they suffer the risks of a lack of asset <u>location</u> diversification. Thus, they're at risk of a large part of their wealth both performing poorly and being subjected to some external event – <u>e.g.</u>, the tax treatment of the 401(k) or college savings plan changing.

As I said earlier, if there were one ideal asset, everyone would just buy it on the Internet. In any individual situation, there are likely to be multiple different investments in play. Thus, the strategy one has should take into account the benefits of and interrelationship among different assets in an allocation. But, just for fun, when I ask my clients to catalog characteristics of the ideal investment, they most often include:

- A reasonable expected rate of return (taking into account fees/expenses)
- An amount of risk commensurate with the expected rate of return
- Favorable tax treatment
- Transparency regarding how the investment works
- Ease of accessing it

And then I sometimes add:

- Simplicity and regularity of adding to it
- Unaffected in the event of one's disability or death
- Protection from creditors
- A reliable source of retirement income/a good "nest egg"
- Ease of passing on to heirs, charities, etc.

Working with your advisor, you can use the above list as a starting point to "test" the various possibilities and see how they stack up, including:

- Individual stocks
- Individual bonds
- Mutual funds of stocks and/or bonds
- Real estate
- Business ownership
- Life insurance

It's likely you'll find merit in more than one of these asset types (and likely others as well). Also, you'll see I included life insurance in this list. Although some might consider it "uncommon" to find in a list of assets, I believe the discussions regarding the attributes and use of life insurance in Chapters 4 and 8 make it a strong contender here.

I'm tempted to offer some "warnings" relating to asset recommendations you come across (e.g., watch out for advice that "now is the time to get into soybeans" - or whatever). However, that's not the point of this book (and, if it were, the book would be twice as long!). Rather, my suggestion is to keep the following simple points in mind when assessing any such recommendation:

- Is it based on sound, verifiable facts or on emotion, salesmanship or guesswork (even if it's educated guesswork)?

- How and where does it fit within your risk tolerance and asset allocation?
- Does it line up with enough of the attributes you've identified of an "ideal" asset to make sense?

Tax-Advantaged Growth Vehicles

You'll notice that things like annuities, 401(k)s and Section 529 college savings plans are missing from the above list – that's because to a large extent they are tax vehicles, not assets – although they may be made up of assets like mutual funds.[8] A general thought about those vehicles: they're all at risk of changes in the tax law – perhaps now more than ever in the past given the growing budget deficits. There's some reason to hope that any changes will be prospective only but no guaranty of that. Thus, that's another argument for diversification – maybe not everything with favorable tax treatment will be hit or hit as badly. For instance, I'd argue that assets like real estate and life insurance, which have enjoyed their tax benefits throughout most of the history of the tax laws, may be more "solid" than much-newer 401(k)s and 529 plans, which are purely creatures of tax law.

Let's discuss annuities, 401(k)s and 529 plans in a little depth because all three are very popular and can play a role in one's growth portfolio but also are somewhat misunderstood.

Annuities

Annuities enable one to effectively create her own private pension plan. They come in two general types. There are immediate annuities and deferred annuities. With immediate

---

[8] Some may question why life insurance is not also considered simply a tax vehicle – that's because, while it has tax deferral features, it also is an asset class in and of itself, not just a vehicle or chassis for other assets.

annuities you deposit a lump sum of money with an annuity issuer and are paid a stream of income starting today that is guaranteed to last either for a set period of time or for your (and your spouse's if you so choose) entire life. The longer the guaranteed stream, the lower the payment you receive and, if you die after you start receiving payments, typically the payments stop and the issuer of the annuity keeps the remaining money. With the <u>deferred</u> annuity, one deposits money with the issuer today, the money is invested by the issuer or by you (depending on the specific type), grows tax-deferred and at some point in the future you (or, again, your spouse in some instances) turn on a stream of payments based on the value the annuity has grown to during the deferral (or what's called the "accumulation") period.

Annuities, particularly the ones that are deferred where you direct the investment of the funds (what are called "deferred variable annuities") have had a checkered history, to say the least. That's partly attributable to some earlier product features and partly due to bad sales practices. Unfortunately, that history has caused many (particularly the "sound bite," "one-size-fits-all" financial entertainers in the media) to throw the variable annuity baby out with the bathwater. I want to spend a little more time on deferred variable annuities because, used in the right way in the right circumstances, they can be a very powerful tool. I'm speaking in particular of ones that have a guaranteed growth component - e.g., the value of the annuity grows at least by a minimum amount - and a guarantee regarding the minimum stream of income that can be taken from that guaranteed growth.

There are many aspects of annuities to be cognizant of – there may be charges and/or penalties for taking money out early; withdrawals can have the effect of reducing benefits under the annuity; there are a myriad of fees; the tax treatment is not that favorable; and one is exposed to the risk of the financial strength of the issuer of the annuity. These and other features typically are pointed to as making deferred variable annuities "bad investments." Here are my shorthand responses to these points, and more:

▶ "<u>You have to lock your money up for a long time or else you get penalized.</u>" It is true there are IRS penalties (as there are with 401(k)s or IRAs) for early withdrawals, as well as potential charges by the annuity issuer (depending on the particular annuity and when and how much money is taken out) but the money IS accessible – some of it or all of it. Taking money out could, however, have an impact on the valuable guarantees that were the reason to purchase the annuity to begin with. Thus, the relevant point is you shouldn't be DOING an annuity with any money where there's a meaningful chance you'll need to access it soon.

▶ "<u>There are high fees in variable annuities and you could do better with the same investments outside the annuity.</u>" These fees are in part for the management of the mutual fund-like vehicles in which the owner of the annuity (you) invests the money deposited. It is true those fees can be higher than in other mutual funds that are not part of an annuity – but not always so. Further, a chunk of the fees have nothing to do with the investments – they have to do with the guarantees associated with the annuity structure, which you certainly are not getting in other plain vanilla mutual fund investments. Again, one should be putting funds into a variable annuity for the guaranteed growth and guaranteed income features – those are not affected by fees at all. The fees may mean that your core investment (which is the money you could walk away with if you terminated the annuity instead of waiting to take advantage of the guaranteed amounts) may be eaten away if the investments don't do very well but, again, don't use a variable annuity if your intention is to access it soon.

- ▶ "The money is at risk if the annuity issuer goes out of business." That is true to a certain extent – there are state guarantee funds that would provide some protection but the bigger factor to rely on is doing business with an annuity issuer that has high financial ratings and a long history in business.

- ▶ "The guaranteed growth and income amounts may be harmed by high inflation." Although it is true that the growth and income guarantees of most (not all) variable annuities today are fixed and thus at risk of inflation, one should assess whether the fact of those guarantees nevertheless makes the risk worth taking for a portion of their retirement assets.

- ▶ "The insurance company gets to keep the remaining money when I die, which particularly stinks if I die soon." This generally is not true with modern-day deferred variable annuities.

- ▶ "The tax treatment of money in an annuity is less favorable than other alternatives." This is true – just as with pension plan or 401(k) money, although income is not taxed until distributions are taken, such distributions are taxed at ordinary income, rather than lower capital gains, rates. In addition, annuities, like 401(k)s and IRAs, are treated less favorably than other assets when inherited. Certainly, those factors can be a disadvantage (as is the general risk of tax deferral discussed in Chapter 5 and later in this Chapter). Again, these points have to be balanced against the benefit of the guarantees. Further, if existing IRA or 401(k) money is used in an annuity because of the appeal of its guarantees, then the tax treatment is identical under current law.

I think the above items should help show that for a portion of one's assets – and particularly that which you don't intend to touch for a while and would like to turn into a piece of the guaranteed foundation of your retirement income – annuities can play a valuable role. Because, really, **there is NOTHING else – other than things like FDIC-insured CDs and life insurance with guarantees – that can secure the growth and distribution of money to the same extent**. Everything else has some degree of risk – potentially lower cost and greater rewards, yes – but greater risk and the goal here is to reduce that risk as to a meaningful portion of your retirement income. There are, however, a lot of variable annuity products out there and they have a myriad of features that make them very complicated. Thus, after you rid yourself of any remaining bias against variable annuities, this is another area where it's important to have an advisor who can guide you through.

401(k)s (or any "tax-qualified" retirement plan)

These are vehicles where money is invested before tax, grows without tax and then is fully taxed when withdrawn.[9] Let's be crystal clear – **there IS NO tax savings associated with plans like these. What there is is TAX DEFERRAL.** In exchange for keeping your money invested on a pre-tax

---

[9] Roth IRAs and Roth 401(k)s differ in that funds are invested after-tax, grow without tax and can be taken out without tax. The availability of those vehicles to many people is limited by income or plan design. However, when available, compared to pre-tax vehicles, they may be a better "bet" given the risks of future taxation described in this Chapter. On the other hand, they still require locking up your money for some time and hoping that the tax treatment doesn't change between now and retirement. There are other ways worth exploring to save money on an after-tax basis and be able to access it without tax in the future.

basis, eventually the government wants its share of 100% of the money that's been invested and the earnings on it. And the government wants the money at much higher ordinary income, rather than capital gains, tax rates. Further, as we learned in Chapter 5 about the history of taxes, **any hope that those rates will be lower in the future when the money is taken out is very thin.** While there is a benefit to deferring taxation until money is withdrawn, that benefit may not be large enough to offset the risk of higher taxation compared to other available investment alternatives.

Let's think about who likes these "tax-qualified" vehicles (meaning they're "qualified" under the Internal Revenue Code to not require current taxation). Number one, the government likes them because it takes the pressure off of the Social Security system and also provides a handy vehicle (you!) to take care of investing and growing the tax dollars you're going to pay down the road. Number two, the big investment companies like them because they get an easy, regular flow of new investment dollars. Finally, your accountant/CPA/financial advisor likes them because he gets to be a hero by "reducing" your taxes today by recommending them and is unlikely to be on the scene decades from now when you start taking the money out and cursing the taxes you're paying!

I'd add that most other investment alternatives also don't entail the loss of control that tax-deferred retirement plans do – like the annuities described earlier, one can't remove money from those plans without penalty until they're 59½ years old. To add further to the doom and gloom, it also seems inevitable that the tax law writers are going to have to delay that age even further – perhaps to the mid or late 60's - because they can't afford to incent folks to retire early and stop contributions from their employment income to Medicare and Social Security.

Now, I'm not saying not to fund 401(k)s and similar plans if there's an employer match – but funding them above the amount necessary to receive the maximum employer match is, I'd argue, a very questionable strategy. And, even if you could get a match, if you're contributing money to these accounts and thus putting it at risk before you've done the things outlined earlier in this book to protect your money, I'd question whether that's prudent. (An employer match or a little tax-deferred growth today can't possibly make up for being disabled for the rest of your life and having inadequate disability income insurance, for instance.)

Whether or not you "max out" your qualified plan contributions, I want to be sure you have the right perspective about your account – it's like one of those distorting mirrors – amounts in the 401(k) are smaller than they appear – perhaps by 30, 40 or 50% or more after the tax hit is factored in. Plus, think about your tax situation when you plan to take the money out – not only may you be in a similar or higher tax bracket as today, you're likely going to have fewer deductions to offset tax – less mortgage interest deduction, fewer dependents. And, further, you can't escape the tax by just passing the money on at death - unlike other inherited money, 401(k) and IRA money cannot escape taxation when inherited.

Section 529 College Savings Plans

"Saving for college" is not an investment per se; it's a "goal" like retirement. Nevertheless, it almost always comes up when speaking of investments. Let me start by saying that I have nothing against saving for your children's college education if you so desire – that's great. My concern is WHERE you save. 529 plans are named after Section 529 of the Internal Revenue Code - technically they're called "qualified tuition plans" but, because they essentially only can be used for college tuition, they're usually called "college savings plans". They are touted as great college savings vehicles because, while the money goes in after tax, it grows without tax and can be used in limited circumstances without tax.

Usually, the focus around 529 plans is assessing which state's plan to use (each state sponsors its own plan). Unless you're participating in what's call a "prepaid" college savings plan where the state guarantees you a certain tuition rate at its state's schools, 529 money can be used at any college or university anywhere.[10] Different states have different plan providers and choices and there sometimes is a small state income tax benefit for setting up a 529 account under the plan of the state in which you live. In the "advice" I see out there, there's generally no analysis of the merits of using the 529 to begin with – it's just assumed because it's called a "college savings plan" that that's what one is supposed to use. Here are some factors to consider before devoting money to a 529 plan:

> ▶ Age of Children. If 529s make sense at all, it's only when you have young children and, thus, a good chunk of time to benefit from the tax-free growth of the money. But, really, if you have a five year old, do you want to be deciding 13 or more years ahead of time that he or she IS going to college and that the best way to pay for his or her college at that time is going to be to use your cash? Because that's what you're doing with the 529. The money can be used for another child or grandchild (or you!) if it turns out

---

[10] Money in a "prepaid" plan can be used at schools outside the state, but the tuition guaranty would not apply (nor would the money deposited be credited with any meaningful growth). I also would caution that, in several states, the tuition "guaranty" is not backed by the full faith and credit of the state; rather, it's dependent on there being enough funds in the state's overall plan to cover the tuition obligations at any point in time.

not to be used for the original child but that's not why you put the money in to begin with, was it?

- ▶ Mandatory Use. If in 13 (or whatever) years there's some government program you or your child can take advantage of to pay for college or if there's some borrowing you or the child can do to pay for college that is desirable, you'll be reluctant to do so if you have a lot of 529 money to spend. Even today there are options to borrow the money, keep your other money working for you and take advantage of inflation by paying the loan back years from now with deflated dollars.

- ▶ Financial Aid Impact. You may not be counting on receiving financial aid for your child but if you're going to want to save up a slug of money to have potentially to use for college, wouldn't it be better to save it in a place that's not visible for college financial aid qualification calculation purposes rather than in a very obvious "college savings plan"?

- ▶ Other Opportunities. With the 529 you have no other use of the money for yourself or for the prospective college student who may turn out to be an Internet genius and need money for a startup business more than she needs it for college tuition!

- ▶ You First. And, how about if things don't go so well for you and YOU need the money that went into the 529 to live on? You may have heard the caveat: you can borrow for college but you can't borrow for retirement. It'd be a sad state of affairs if your child is navigating the food court at an Ivy league school while you're navigating the day-old section of your local grocery store!

- ▶ Investment Risk. Is a potentially volatile investment account the best place to save for college? Almost by definition it only makes sense if the money in the 529 account is put at risk in the market – how about if (as has happened of late) it's substantially diminished at the very time it's needed?

- ▶ Tax Risk. In the context of tax laws, 529 plans have been around for a nanosecond. As a practical matter, they mostly benefit the top echelon (the supposed "rich") in society. It may be risky to assume their favorable tax treatment will be preserved into the future.

- ▶ Other Risks. Again, as with 401(k)s, do not put money in 529 plans until you're protected from liability, sickness and premature death. The whole college plan could be disrupted if one of these scenarios occurs.

My clients know I'm leery of 529 accounts. Nevertheless, if they want to put a modest amount of money there (on the assumption a lot more money will be needed for college from some other source), I don't throw my body in front of them. I just want people to go in with eyes open to the price to be paid in exchange for the benefits of 529 plans. At the same time, it's important to consider whether other vehicles can serve the same purpose – for instance, just because investment real estate is not called a "college savings plan" doesn't mean that it couldn't serve that purpose, with more benefits, more flexibility and you may even be able to visit it on vacation a couple weeks a year – you can't do that with a 529 plan!

In general, the best plan for paying for college is to use what we call "OPM" (for, "Other Peoples' Money"). Whether it's grants, scholarships or loans, the idea is to preserve your own capital to grow and be used as you wish. Of course, college is a great investment for your kids - it's just not such a great investment for you, which makes the cash you use to pay for it probably the most significant lost opportunity cost you'll ever experience (unless you count on saving nursing home costs because paying for college will encourage your kids to take care of you in your old age!).

One final word on saving for college: another place it's done is in accounts that are creatures of state law called "Uniform Transfers to Minors Act" or "Uniform Gifts to Minors Act" (abbreviated as "UTMA" or "UGMA") accounts. Although these accounts don't carry the same tax benefit that 529 plans do, sometimes they're used because it seems like a nice, clearly-dedicated place to save and has greater investment flexibility than a 529 account; sometimes it's done because there can be a little tax savings (some of the earnings can be taxed at the child's lower tax rate). Any advantages, however, may be outweighed by the fact that this money is the child's money once deposited; the child has unencumbered control over it at age 18 or 21 (depending on the state's law); and it can have a significant impact on any chance to qualify for college financial aid.[11]

Investing Style

Let's refer back for a moment to the asset allocation implementation discussion earlier in this Chapter. At least as

---

[11] There also are more complex methods to save money for children – e.g., trusts that are established for their benefit by a parent or grandparent. These can provide for more control than UTMA/UGMA accounts but my concern with such trusts is that the cost to establish and administer them (and the limitations that exist on the use of the money) may outweigh their benefits. Also, it's worth noting that parents, grandparents and others can give an unlimited amount of money outside the transfer tax system if it's paid directly to the provider of educational (or medical) services.

to the traditional stocks/bonds/mutual funds part of your allocation, you'll have to make a basic philosophical choice between investing via an "active" approach (that is, where you - directly, through an advisor or through institutional managers, such as in mutual funds - try to be smart about stock or bond picking) or via a "passive" approach (that is, where you choose non-actively managed investments such as funds that more or less mechanistically track publicly-available market indices) to complete your asset allocation. You'd take the latter route if you subscribe to the "efficient markets hypothesis" – which holds that information regarding investments is quickly and pervasively disseminated, it's difficult for even very smart people to consistently beat the overall averages of market performance, and it's costly to try in the hope that there some day may be a "home run."

You'd take the active route if you think smart people can outsmart the general direction of the market on a consistent basis and do so to a sufficient extent to offset the higher costs of such an approach. (I've also seen situations where someone ends up with a mixture of active and passive investments – that tells me either that there is not a clear understanding of what investment strategy is being followed and/or someone is trying to hedge his bets between whether the active or passive approach is best.) If you're in the "active" camp, however, I would encourage you NOT to chase the manager, fund, stock, whatever, that was "hot" last year (have you noticed that the annual Money magazine "hottest funds of the year" list often is entirely different every year?). That approach will be both frustrating and futile.

There is no absolute right answer here (otherwise, again, if there were everyone would just do that) and it is beyond the scope of this book to lay out all the pros and cons of investing styles. The good news, as described above, is that this part of the investment strategy is of far less importance than the overall asset allocation you choose. Nevertheless, with whom or what you complete your asset allocation can't be ignored. Further, because allocation is so important in performance, you want to get it done as effectively as possible. In making that decision I suggest you focus not on quarter-to-quarter or year-to-year performance but on long-term (as in five or ten years) performance, costs and, most importantly: process. **That is, what's the most precise way to implement and maintain your asset allocation, at the lowest cost, with the best long-term performance?**

Putting It All Together

What I've outlined above is the antithesis of the ad hoc, sound bite investment/asset decision making most people engage in – they buy "this" mutual fund, "that" hot stock, throw a dart to make their 401(k) choices, and so on. **Thus, again, if you can put aside fears of meltdown/Armageddon, the existence of an overarching, objective, scientific strategy should provide the maximum confidence possible when navigating the always rocky investment waters.** I hasten to add, however, that all this Chapter does is provide a roadmap to traditional tactical decisions involving acquiring stocks/bonds/mutual funds. It gets you to a place where you have the best chance of achieving reasonable growth over the long-term for the risk you're willing and able to take. However, unless it also gets you to the point where you have "more money than God" (a technical financial term!), it does not get you where you really need to be – which is **to be comfortable spending as much of your wealth as possible during retirement without fear of running out before you die (or before you're able to pass something on to others if you so desire).**

In order to accomplish the above objective, **ideally you'll have one or more "permission slip" assets in place.**

What's a "permission slip" asset? It's an asset that has low volatility (that is, a low standard deviation from its projected return – even better if it has guarantees associated with it) and has a return that is uncorrelated to the greatest extent possible to the performance of other assets you have (meaning it goes up in value when others go down). Examples of such an asset are real estate (although the experience of the past few years has shown these things not to be as true about real estate as in the past) and cash value (or whole) life insurance (where the experience of the past few years has shown these things to be truer than most anyone previously understood).

What's the point of having a "permission slip" asset? We'll discuss that in more detail in the next Chapter but, in summary, having a permission slip asset in place truly allows those <u>without</u> more money than God to "have their cake and eat it too". That is because they know that, with the permission slip asset sitting in the background, they have the "permission" to spend their other assets liberally. In the event they run out of those other assets (either because they had to spend them or just used them for fun, good works, whatever), they (and/or eventually their heirs) will have the permission slip asset to rely on.

A Friendly Caveat

I mentioned earlier the "do it yourself" approach. As with other financial areas, in my experience very few people are capable of doing the investment thing themselves correctly. Certainly, if you want to keep a little stash of "fun money" to play the market and you (and anyone who cares about your money, like your spouse) are fine if you lose it all, go for it. As to your overall integrated investment portfolio, devoting the attention to making the right initial choices, continually monitoring those choices, doing the necessary rebalancing and assessing factors like tax implications is something that, even if you <u>could</u> and <u>would</u> do it, is likely not worth your time.

Thus, I think this is a realm where it pays to pay. I have a client who, when he thought about the fees that working with me on his investments entailed, concluded that my advice was worth at least what he paid his maid. So, although I'm sorry, for my sake, that he apparently was paying his maid more than me on an annual basis, it's a nice way to think about it – just as he didn't want to deal with the mess and time of cleaning his house and was willing to pay someone to do that, so was he willing to pay me and my firm because he saw I could do a better job, more efficiently – just like his maid!

Uncommon Takeaways

- ▶ Ignore investment products until you have an investment strategy.

- ▶ In developing that strategy, don't overestimate your risk tolerance.

- ▶ Don't become enamored with factors that don't significantly enhance long-term performance – such as trying to pick "hot" assets or "time" the market – as opposed to asset allocation.

- ▶ Make sure you apply objective standards to deciding upon assets that will be part of your asset allocation and that they fit the investing "style" you are comfortable with.

- ▶ Don't automatically rule out tax vehicles like annuities but do carefully weigh their pros and cons and compare them to other alternatives.

- ▶ Make sure you haven't put too many eggs in any one asset basket and that your mix of assets when you reach retirement will enable you to have the greatest possible spendability from the money you've accumulated.

- ▶ Please be honest: are you really going to be able to "do it yourself?" And is that approach really in your and your family's best interest?

CAPPING IT OFF: USING YOUR MONEY

Chapter 8. Money and Its Use

"You're called 'boomers' because 'boom' is the sound most of you will make when you crash into your retirement years."

This is where, as they say, the rubber hits the road and, of course, no one wants to hear the "boom" sound! If you've done the right things to protect and grow your money, you eventually arrive at a point where you have money and need or want to use it because your earned income (such as a salary) has stopped or is not sufficient by itself to bear the cost of what you want or need to spend. This could be college tuition, it could be long-term care for you or your spouse, it could be just to live life in retirement or (hopefully) it could be fun things like vacations, boats, country clubs, convertibles, and so on! **I think most people would say their goal for their money at this point is to get the most enjoyment possible out of it, without fearing running out prior to death, and then pass on a legacy to family, charities, and so on.**

How Much Do I Need?

There's a popular book and a financial institution advertising campaign tied into the concept of the amount of money one needs to live in retirement – which some call their "number." Honestly, for all the hype around this, I've never found anyone who actually has reached retirement who particularly cares what their "number" turned out to be. I understand it might have some significance from a bragging rights standpoint to have a "big" number. The relevant question for people at this point, however, is: **"how much can I/we spend this year, next year, and so on without running out before I/we die?"**

And that's how it should be – you can't "spend" your "number" – all you can do is add it up on a piece of paper!

And Why It's Not Enough

The brutal truth is that, no matter how well they plan, the "number" most people (including those earning very healthy salaries now) will end up with is not going to be enough to permit them to spend with abandon (those <u>without</u> "more money than God" referred to in the last Chapter). Here's the "harsh" reality – given ever-increasing lifespans the average healthy professional person who retires at age 65 (and/or his spouse) may have 20 – 30 or more years to live in retirement. The cost of that, coupled with the impact of market volatility or of low investment returns in order to avoid market volatility, as well as all the "headwinds" I described in Chapter 5 (particularly the loss of purchasing power due to inflation), is what explains the train wreck most people are headed for. Why are they on this path? For many varied reasons but I think two key ones are:

1. **They simply didn't save enough when times were green (and its cousin: they spent too much).** This

is, for example, the person who envisioned that at retirement he'd have $1,000,000 saved up. We'll talk about what that $1,000,000 could do for him later on but, first, what IS $1,000,000? Well, even at this writing it's not what it used to be. But if our envisioner currently is 45 years old, when he or she is 65 that $1,000,000 will feel like $553,700 if we compute 20 years' worth of only 3% annual inflation. And then by the time he is 95 and there have been another 30 years of 3% inflation, that $1,000,000 will feel like only $228,100. (Or, if you want to think about it from the other direction, a condo that costs $228,100 today will cost $1 million 50 years from now, at a 3% growth rate!)

2. **They've saved in the wrong places and it has experienced market volatility, low growth or high taxes.** An example of this is the person who took the financial entertainers' advice to "before you do anything else, max out your 401(k) and/or IRA" and who was proud to enter retirement with a $1,000,000 retirement account only to find that (separate and apart from the inflation issue above!) he really only has something like $500,000 after factoring in the Federal, state and local taxes that likely will eat into that $1,000,000 pot of money that never has been taxed! Another example is the pursuit of the almighty rate of return and the hope people have that that will bail them out of a sparse retirement. They are enthralled by the theoretical potential average returns based on long-term historical figures that, while numerically accurate, are not real in that few actual investors ever achieve them. That's because either their investment horizon is different from the average and/or they can't stick with the program and make the "buy high" and "sell low" mistake too often.

Let's look at the "why it's not enough" point from another angle. Assume you're 40 years old today and making $100,000 a year.[12] You hope you'll be fortunate enough to receive, on average, 5% raises for the next 25 years until retirement. That means at retirement you'll be making $338,600 a year. And, let's assume you gradually became used to making $338,600 a year too! Then, you retire and some pundits say you'll be able to live on 80% of your final income. (I'd say that's probably the bare minimum – no one (unless they HAVE to) finds that all of a sudden their spending drops meaningfully after retirement, other than for things like 401(k) contributions.) At 80%, you need $270,900 a year to live for the next – what? – 20 years – in retirement before you and your spouse die. If we assume you can live with that $270,900 being deflated by inflation over those 20 years and could find somewhere to put the money during that time where it didn't lose value and maybe could earn 4% year in and year out (perhaps a generous assumption), you'd need a pot of money at retirement of $3,750,000 to generate that $270,900 a year for 20 years until it runs out (of course, not counting any Social Security or other guaranteed income you receive). If you factor in inflation continuing at its 3% long-run average and you want to take more than that $270,900 each year to keep up an after-inflation cash flow that stays equivalent to the original $270,900, that means you'd need a pot of $4,750,000.

I'm assuming your "pot" is money will not need to be taxed (other than on the ongoing 4% it makes) when you take it out – which is not likely since a lot of that money probably will be retirement plan distributions – but I don't want to depress you any more. And, of course, the even bigger problem is you don't know that you and your spouse both will be around for only 20 more years – you might be around 30 or 40 more years. Plus, you don't necessarily want to die broke and leave no legacy, so

---

[12] And, trust me, the results described here tend to be no different if one is making $500,000 a year at age 40!

even if you have the necessary pot of money at retirement, you can't spend it down to zero over 20 years for fear of running out.

There are a myriad of books, articles, etc. from the media and mass market financial institutions that purport to provide practical guidance on how to deal with this situation. The guidance most often is rather obvious (or should I say "common?"): that you need to spend less, work longer, save more and, worst of all, take more risk with your retirement savings. And, what they lay out is based on a slew of assumptions and guesswork about what amount you'll "need" in retirement, how long you'll live in retirement, what your market returns will be, what inflation and taxes will be, and on and on. To me, the greatest flaws are that they assume average historical rates of return will be your rate of return and, basically, that life will proceed in a nice, linear fashion, which of course does not happen. **What they are all lacking is a real strategy that can reduce the dependence on all these variables turning out "right."**

I believe the strategy I need to assist my clients to implement now is one that helps them get the most what we call "spendability" out of the precious assets they have (including, if possible and desired, enabling them to give money away before or after their death). And we cannot, despite all our cool technology, figure out how to implement the goal espoused by the current Mayor of New York City and one of the wealthiest men in the world (who I hasten to add has no reason to worry about his "number"!) that the check to the undertaker bounce! So, assuming you're not on the Forbes magazine billionaire list, let's look at the nuts and bolts of how retirement could play out.

Guaranteed Retirement Income

The analysis of the use of money in retirement starts with the amount of "guaranteed" income one has – that includes

Social Security and any employer pension plans (understanding that neither of these really is absolutely guaranteed – but let's agree that, in this world, they come as close as reasonably possible to guaranteed). Social Security currently is intended to keep up with the cost of living, at least to some extent; pension plans typically have a static payout that does not increase. And, of course, the sum of both is not likely to be anywhere near what one needs to live through a long retirement.

As discussed earlier in the Money and Growth Chapter, you may have set up an additional guaranteed stream of income by purchasing a deferred variable annuity that has grown for a number of years and can be "turned on" to generate payments for the remainder of one or both spouses' lives. Instead of (or in addition to) the variable annuity, it is possible to use some of your retirement assets and purchase an immediate annuity at or after retirement, which will start a stream of payments (again, guaranteed potentially for both spouses' lives). Either way, these are like private pension plans that, while there are both pros and cons to consider, may be appropriate to put in place for a portion of one's wealth to further shore up the guaranteed retirement income foundation. Finally, a traditional use of cash value life insurance is to generate tax-free distributions (when properly structured) from it to supplement retirement income. Although that's certainly a possibility, we'll shortly discuss strategies that will make you want to keep that as among the last of the assets you'll touch.

The Rest of the Story

Now, let's focus on where the rest of your retirement income – beyond what's guaranteed – will come from.

Although with the first of the baby boomers reaching retirement age there's been a lot of talk about strategies for distributing one's wealth in retirement, most investment managers aren't too keen on that because they make money from the amount of assets they buy and manage for you and, clearly, distribution is going in the wrong direction for them. Further, distribution is a dicey proposition – if you assume your account value is static or rising, it's fairly easy to approximate how long one's money may last based on a specific withdrawal amount each year – and guessing how much longer you and your spouse are going to live. Unfortunately, we don't know our lifespans and most people will live "too long" and don't have enough money saved to be able to simply live on their pile of money in retirement. That leads to perhaps the greatest flaw in common financial planning – that is, that retirement has to be deferred or limited and/or retirement assets have to be put at greater market risk; of course, that means trouble.

You'll recall in our example earlier that I assumed a constant 4% rate of return on retirement income. That'd be ideal because there's nothing quite so devastating as withdrawing money from an account while it is simultaneously going down in value. The chart below shows the real life impact of taking $80,000 a year out of a $1,000,000 account starting in 1995 when the market was going up vs. starting in 2000 when the market was going down – not a pretty picture and particularly frustrating because, of course, it's not possible to know with certainty when you begin retirement which of the scenarios is going to be your scenario!

Year	S&P 500 Return	Beg. Year Value	Annual Distrib.	End Year Value
1995	37.56%	$1,000,000	$80,000	$1,265,552
1996	22.90%	$1,265,552	$80,000	$1,457,043
1997	33.34%	$1,457,043	$80,000	$1,836,150
1998	28.58%	$1,836,150	$80,000	$2,258,057
1999	21.01%	$2,258,057	$80,000	$2,635,667
2000	-9.11%	$1,000,000	$80,000	$836,188
2001	-11.90%	$836,188	$80,000	$666,202
2002	-22.14%	$666,202	$80,000	$456,417
2003	28.62%	$456,417	$80,000	$484,147
2004	11.01%	$484,147	$80,000	$448,644

Source: Pinnacle Data Corporation

Some money management professionals try to get smarter about predicting how much money safely can be withdrawn during retirement despite variability in investment returns by interposing what's called a "Monte Carlo" analysis. The "Monte Carlo" part relates to making bets as they do in that high-flying town near the coast of southern France known for its high-stakes gambling – that alone should give you some pause about relying on it too heavily. It's appalling that, in the absence of anything more solid, many professionals treat the Monte Carlo analysis as sufficient. Taken with enough grains of salt, however, it can be illuminating. What it does is take a specific investment pot of money and run hundreds or thousands of potential scenarios of market performance – in terms of up years and down years in differing amounts and in differing sequences - to assess the average potential chance, expressed as a percentage, that you won't run out of money over a specified time frame as you're taking a specified amount of withdrawals.

You'll find if you have a Monte Carlo analysis done that, unless you start with a big enough pot of money or reduce the time period or the amount of distributions you take, there will be a significant chance you'll run out of money during your expected lifespan and be left living off cat food (and not the good kind either!). And even if you don't completely run out of money, what you have left effectively will have had its purchasing power substantially diminished over time due to inflation. The common advice regarding how to maintain purchasing power is to keep a significant portion of one's money at risk in the equity markets. Over an extended period of time, that theoretically is an effective strategy. I say "theoretically" because it depends on <u>what</u> period of time applies to <u>you</u> (as depicted in the charts above) and whether you can stand the volatility that is the <u>quid pro quo</u> for achieving returns in excess of the inflation rate to preserve purchasing power – most people in retirement simply cannot.

Thus, the only cure is to be able to ensure your retirement pot of money <u>doesn't</u> have to be put at significant risk but can generate sufficient cash flow to enable you to stop working if/when you wish and still have a robust lifestyle, no matter how long you live. We'll talk about how to do that next.

The Permission Slip

My hope is you reach retirement by working with an advisor to save and grow significant wealth and you save and grow it in the right places. And, because I am rooting for, but not counting on, you ending up with more money than God, some of those "right places" should be what we called "permission slip" assets back in Chapter 7. But, as I mentioned in that Chapter, it's critical that there be a strategy for and synergy among the assets you acquire prior to retirement. Although having ONLY a "permission slip" asset might not be devastating, it would be much better to have additional asset location diversification during your accumulation years (so that, perhaps, you can hit a stock market home run!). It will be much more powerful in retirement to have that permission slip asset side-by-side with other assets so that the spendability of those other assets is enhanced by the existence of the permission slip asset. The remainder of this Chapter will review a few examples of the strategies that having permission slip assets enable.[13]

Asset Spending

Scenario 1

Let's assume "Ted" reaches retirement at age 60 with $5 million to spend in retirement. Most people these days would consider that a "success." Then, what does Ted do with that $5 million? The most typical approach is for Ted to look at that $5 million, envision that he and/or his spouse may live for at least another 30 years, during which time the $5 million is going to be decimated by inflation, and conclude that he needs to keep that $5 million invested (probably rather conservatively) and live off the interest income. The table below depicts how that plays out for the time from age 60 to 80 – essentially, $120,000 of after-tax income (before inflation, I might add) to live on based on a 4% rate of return and a 40% Federal, state and local tax bracket. Yes, they might want (or need) to dip into the $5 million principal but, as we discussed earlier, doing so is risky because it means you have to then keep dipping in more and more to keep up the stream of income. And, we've assumed the 4% rate of return happens every year – maybe achievable but by no means guaranteed (also, I wouldn't bet on their tax rate being as low as 40%).

---

[13] If you're at or near retirement without having created a permission slip asset earlier in life, do not despair! By taking a portion of existing assets and using those to create a permission slip asset, you may be able to gain significant additional spendability from the remaining assets while that permission slip asset grows, to be available for use later if necessary.

Year	After-tax Cash Flow	Remaining Value
1	$120,000	$5,000,000
5	$120,000	$5,000,000
10	$120,000	$5,000,000
15	$120,000	$5,000,000
20	$120,000	$5,000,000

Total 20 year cash flow: $2,400,000

In sum, they've been able to spend $2.4 million and still have $5 million left to use from age 80 onward.

Scenario 2

Now, let's envision Ted put in place a permission slip asset (like whole life insurance) at an earlier age. The table below depicts what Ted would be able to do in that situation – that is, use the $5 million retirement pot of money to generate a stream of income that amortizes (like a mortgage) the $5 million down to zero over 20 years. You see that that more than <u>doubles</u> their net after-tax income each year (the amount goes up because the payment is made up of more and more of the original $5 million of principal each year and less and less interest, so there's less tax incurred). **The result is, after 20 years – I might add that it's the 20 years when Ted and his wife are likely to be relatively healthier and want to travel, have more fun, etc. - they've had much more than twice as much money to spend ($6.4 million vs. $2.4 million) as they would have had if they'd had to live off the "interest-only" approach in Scenario 1.**

Year	After-tax Cash Flow	Remaining Value
1	$287,909	$4,832,091
5	$299,317	$4,090,551
10	$316,340	$2,984,067
15	$337,051	$1,637,860
20	$362,249	$0

Total 20 year cash flow: $6,414,909

Oh yes, the "problem" is that Ted and his wife have run out of their $5 million by the 20th year and he's only 80 years old. But, they still have the whole life insurance "permission slip" in place. If they had put $5 million of life insurance in place on Ted at age 45, and paid for it until Ted retired at age 60 (and then just let it grow based on the existing value in it), it's possible (depending on the policy, insurer, Ted's health and other factors) that by age 80 it would have a cash value of about $5 million and a death benefit of about $7 million. So, that's what they'd use for the rest of their lives – including for long-term care purposes if necessary - with the result they even may have some legacy to leave at death.

Scenario 3

But, you point out, that $5 million of whole life insurance would have entailed a significant investment and Ted and his wife wouldn't have ended up with $5 million in assets if they had had to buy the whole life insurance. OK, let's assume Ted didn't have approximately $93,600 a year (the theoretical whole life insurance premium) to invest for 15 years that he otherwise could have made 5% on each year after tax. In that case, Ted and his wife would have $2,120,000 less in their retirement "pot" at age 60 than they otherwise would have had. The chart below depicts how, even then, in the "spending" side of the example, Ted and his wife STILL would have had more fun in retirement because of the greater "spendability" of their $2,880,000 (basically, tens of thousands of dollars more each year and 50% more in total - $3.7 million vs. $2.4 million). And, again, at age 80, Ted and his wife are projected to have $5 million of cash value in life insurance they could access. I think this is what is called a "win-win" result.

	$5 million, interest-only		$2,880,000, spending	
Year	After-tax Cash Flow	Remaining Value	After-tax Cash Flow	Remaining Value
1	$120,000	$5,000,000	$165,835	$2,783,285
5	$120,000	$5,000,000	$172,406	$2,356,160
10	$120,000	$5,000,000	$182,211	$1,718,829
15	$120,000	$5,000,000	$194,141	$943,418
20	$120,000	$5,000,000	$208,655	$0

Total 20 year cash flow: $2,400,000 $3,694,975

<u>Maximizing Your Retirement Plan Payments</u>

How about another one? Say you're fortunate enough to have worked for an employer with an old-style non-contributory pension plan. If you haven't already noticed, when you reach retirement you'll be required to make a decision about whether you want to take those pension payments for your lifetime only (a "single-life" payout) or take a lower payment during your lifetime but have that lower payment continue for your spouse after your death (a "joint and survivor" payout). The amount of the lower payment varies – but it can be 10% or more lower. Most retirees simply have no choice – they've got to take the option with the lower payment so their spouse has something to live on if the retiree dies first. Of course, that's a huge gamble. For instance, my father retired after many years of service in the Federal government. He was about eight years older than my mother and his Civil Service pension was an important part of their retirement income. Thus, he took the lower joint and survivor payout. Well, my father is still going strong at age 91 and my mother died almost 20 years ago.

If my father had had a permission slip asset like permanent life insurance in place when he retired, he would at least have had the option of taking the single-life pension payment. And, if the longevity results had played out "correctly" and he died first, my mother would have had a chunk of life insurance proceeds flow in to provide her the income she needed in place of the pension. These aren't the right numbers but let's assume my father's annual pension was $45,000 and it would have been $50,000 if he'd taken the single-life payout. From a pure economic standpoint, if he'd had that $5,000 difference to invest each year for the 15 years between his retirement and my mother's death and then for the 20 years since her death and could have made 5% on that money, then the real economic cost of the pension decision that he had to make was about $475,000. (Sorry Dad!)[14]

Living On (and In) Your House

Another example: One of the frequent sources of tension in a family is what to do about the family home – mom and dad want to live in it for as long as possible and they'd like to preserve it (or its value) to pass on to their kids. That leads

---

[14] This strategy also can apply to deciding whether to take Social Security income early – normally that's a risky approach because it can forever lock your spouse into a lower Social Security annuity after your death (if you were the higher income earner). However, if the spouse has life insurance to look forward to, it may make sense to go ahead and turn on the Social Security spigot early.

the parents to resist a strategy such as a reverse mortgage because it can eat into the equity in the house. Nevertheless, although there are pros and cons to reverse mortgages, they can provide substantial tax-free income during the parents' lifetime. I'm not talking about income they need to just barely survive – I'm talking about income that can make them comfortable taking another month-long cruise this year (for instance). That would be anathema to many people but, again, if they have a permission slip asset in place, then why not take advantage of the reverse mortgage strategy – get as much income as they can for as long as they live and, when they die, well . . . the permission slip asset is there to pay off the reverse mortgage for the kids if they really want the house or (perhaps more realistically) the lender gets the house and the kids get the permission slip asset and are happy as clams!

Gifting

Here's a final example that was briefly mentioned in an earlier Chapter. One of the distasteful experiences most clients have in retirement is the amount of tax they have to pay when they take money out of their 401(k)s and IRAs (and, we speculated earlier that that tax is only going to get worse in the future). If they have a permission slip asset in place, that should give them the ability (the "permission") to donate some or all of that account to a charity and under current law avoid having to pay tax. Although there's no charitable deduction from gifting this type of asset, who cares – if you're able to generate sufficient spendability from your other assets because there's a permission slip asset to fall back on for you and your kids if those other assets run out, you can squeak past the tax sword of Damocles hanging over your IRA, do something good during your life for a cause you care about and enjoy meaningful participation (charity dinners, board of trustees membership, etc.) that you won't be able to do if you wait for your estate to make a donation after your death!

The Moral of the Story

I have no idea which (or any) of the above scenarios may apply in any particular client situation. What I DO know, however, is if your retirement assets aren't virtually unlimited and if you don't have a permission slip asset in place, the <u>only</u> strategy you're going to practically-speaking have available to you is the one described as Scenario 1 above that basically entails "clipping coupons" (hopefully just the interest and dividend kind and not the grocery store kind unless that's your idea of fun). So, on the assumption you'd prefer having the above alternatives, are your permission slip assets in place?

If one of those permission slips is whole life insurance, you can see how that attribute is another of its "Swiss Army knife" features. I alluded earlier to there being a rationale for creating a whole life insurance asset even beyond the rate of return on its cash value and the fact that it saves the down the drain term insurance premium and related lost opportunity costs. To illustrate this – go back to Scenario 3 above where Ted and his wife are able to spend on average about $60,000 a year more, after-tax, over 20 years based on a smaller retirement pot of money because of the presence of the whole life insurance permission slip. To get that same $60,000 a year additional cash flow without the permission slip in place, their "interest only" retirement pot of money would have to have been about $950,000 greater (then invested at 4% and spent over 20 years). If you add together that amount, the cash value growth and the value of the saved term insurance costs – the <u>true total</u> rate of return on the premiums Ted paid for his life insurance policy is very competitive with just about any investment available.

Uncommon Takeaways

▶ What counts is not the size of your number but the spendability of it.

▶ Don't underestimate what amount of money it can take to live in retirement.

▶ Make sure you've got a solid base of guaranteed income in retirement.

▶ Putting one or more "permission slip" assets in place can make the difference between a modest and a robust retirement lifestyle.

Capping It Off: Using Your Money

Chapter 9. Money and Legacy

Money can do a lot of things – it can provide for basic survival as well as some degree of comfort in living beyond basic survival. It can even provide fun. And it can enable us to further a legacy to represent what we've accomplished during our lives. Just for a moment, let's concentrate on the phrase "*further* a legacy." It probably should go without saying, but the first and foremost legacy we all can leave behind has nothing to do with money – it's about the kind of person we've been, how we've lived during our time here and how we've benefitted others – be they family members, friends, co-workers and even the cleaning people who come to empty the trash in your office while you're still cranking away at 7 or 8pm! So, the legacy that money creates – in the form of outright gifts of it, or of things bought with it or built by it – is icing on the cake. If one plans correctly, that should be achievable icing. But I hasten to add that, if you reach the point where you have the money to achieve the icing but you've never baked the cake, as it were, because you did not focus on the people and things that are fundamental, then you have no foundation for the icing.

The venerable Chinese philosopher Lao Tse, in his Tao Teh King, put it well when he said, "The wise man does not lay up treasures – his riches are within . . . . The more he gives to others, the more he has of his own." And, not to speak for the great Master, but I doubt he meant giving others stuff!

Along these same lines, there's an organization called the "True Wealth Community" that has a process called "Blueprinting" that I think is very powerful and revealing.

Their website is www.truewealthcommunity.com and there's a lot more to it than this but, fundamentally, the Blueprinting process asks you to consider the handful of things that make you the happiest and that you value most in life and/or that you'd focus on if you learned you had only six months to live. Then, it asks you to assess how much time TODAY you are devoting to those things. You won't be surprised when I tell you that there's always a substantial disconnect here. We are more focused on the things that Stephen Covey in his four-part time management matrix in The Seven Habits of Highly Effective People describes as in the realm of "Urgent but Not Important." Sometimes we may be doing the "Urgent and Important" but the "Important" things in that case (e.g., crises in the office) are not of the long-lasting type! We need to focus more on what Covey describes as the "Not Urgent but Important." These are characterized by words like "preparation/planning," "relationship building," and "value clarification."

Whether you pursue the Blueprinting process or take a look at Covey's book, I would encourage you to step out of the day-to-day whirlwind for a few moments and consider what's of real, lasting importance in your life and see if you can redouble your efforts to spend more time on that. I'd suggest that one of those important items if you were dying in six months' time would be to get your financial affairs in order and ensure that your loved ones will be taken care of after you're gone. If so, doesn't it make sense to do that now - just in case you don't *have* six months or, if you do, you'll be able to spend those last six months in a more pleasant way than getting your will done? Not to mention the satisfaction and confidence that should result from knowing you have your affairs in order.

Now, assuming you've given the non-material aspects of your legacy some thought, let's talk more about how to have the ability to achieve a legacy via money. Unless you have "extra" assets or a fundamental commitment to a person, cause or organization so that you'll support it no matter what, I submit you'll be in the mode of "I can't worry about heirs or a legacy; I've got to make it through retirement." Without a permission slip asset in place, you only might be comfortable giving a little bit away or even waiting until your death once you're sure you didn't need to spend it.

If you're charitably inclined, charitable giving at death is fine, but wouldn't the BEST scenario be for you to be comfortable giving away assets during your lifetime? In that way you may be able to derive a tax benefit for yourself and, even more importantly, get the benefit of a "living legacy" by seeing your gift at work and participating directly with the recipient of your legacy. The people you usually see doing that are the mega-rich – because they can give money away during their lives without fear of running out. We want ALL our clients to be able to behave like the mega-rich and have enough money and enough ability to spend that money so they can afford to make lifetime charitable gifts. This is a key rationale behind having a permission slip asset in place as described in Chapter 8.

If the existence of a permission slip asset enables you still to have assets left at your death, then your kids both can inherit some money and also effectively have a second inheritance in the form of your estate's gifts to charities (perhaps via a family foundation the kids run). Ideally, the children themselves then would be able to continue to be involved with the charity (hopefully as one big, happy family unit!) and your legacy can continue with the charity far beyond just your tangible gift.

I hope you can see that, with the right strategies in place, it should be possible to accomplish multiple goals:

- Have a financially robust, enjoyable and care-free retirement;

- Be able to choose to give during your lifetime (and certainly after death) a meaningful amount of wealth to heirs, institutions and causes you care about; and

- Give as little of your wealth to taxing authorities as possible.

I trust it's not even necessary at this point in the book to say this, but the above is not going to happen by chance: you need to take action now to have the strategies in place to create the necessary wealth, protect that wealth and maximize the use it can provide for you and others during your life and then what's available for heirs and worthy causes.

Uncommon Takeaways

- Don't confuse "Earth" wealth with "real" wealth because, without real wealth, Earth wealth is meaningless.

- Even if legacy is not your primary goal, it can and should be if you put the right strategies in place.

A Brief Conclusion

Congratulations on making it to this point in the book! Your reward is a very brief distillation of the "bottom line" of what's been discussed so far:

- ▶ Protect your wealth and your family as fully as possible from bad things happening.

- ▶ Save as much money as possible, as early as possible.

- ▶ Allocate that money to grow in the lowest-volatility, most tax-efficient assets possible.

- ▶ Put strategies in place that will enable you to spend what you've protected, saved and grown to the greatest extent possible and then to pass it on if you wish.

All the best,

Joe Bregil

New York, NY
June 2011

EPILOGUE: CHOOSING HELP

There are a variety of reasons why people do not seek professional assistance with their finances and, if they DO seek it, there are a number of mistakes made in choosing that help.

Why No Help?

Besides the normal issues of no time, too many distractions, etc., for those who DO at least begin the thought process of seeking out financial help, many are derailed by one or more of the following factors:

1. Trust – or, more accurately, lack thereof. The client innately assumes there's more in it for the advisor than for them and there's a barrier of suspicion that many advisors have difficulty overcoming. In particular, the client believes they're going to be "sold" something. It's interesting that we humans have this almost visceral reaction to people we believe may be trying to sell us something. The weird thing is, often what's being "sold" to us is a good thing. Further, when you think about it, almost EVERYONE is "selling" something in one way or another – our dentist, our CPA, etc. But, sometimes we're less aware of or less resistant to this "sale" because the object of the sale is something we really want (like a car) or we perceive the seller wants to help us (like a doctor). The financial advisory relationship, if done correctly, should be no different – you should WANT it and you should VALUE what it can do for you (and typically to get it you don't

even have to hop up on one of those examining tables with the crinkly wax paper protection!).

2. Because it's not a life or death situation like assessing why you're having chest pains and, as I said earlier in the book, it's not rocket science, clients often have their own opinions and biases about financial matters that they let get in the way of trusting and relying on others to help them who, frankly, <u>should</u> know a lot more than the client thinks he knows!

3. Very simply, the client just is confused about what she needs to be doing financially and who does what and how they get paid. As we've discussed, the "noise" from the media can be overwhelming, as is the myriad of "advisors" out there with all sorts of different initials after their names. The people one can get assistance from include:

- A traditional stockbroker
- An insurance agent
- A financial planner
- A wealth manager
- A talk show host

The first two categories just want to sell you something and be done – only the very best will stay in touch (because, typically, they hope to be able to sell you something ELSE). The next two will stay in touch if you keep paying them. The last category actually is not even in the financial advice business – those are the ones I called "financial entertainers" earlier in this book because they are in the entertainment (as in, selling advertising) business. They're fine if you want entertainment but I'd only act on what they say if you're also the kind of person who'd base a complicated medical decision on what you hear on TV!

How to Choose Help

I'm sorry to say that the bottom line is it's possible to be poorly advised and even harmed by each and every one of the above categories. Here are a few hints to help ensure you'll have a positive relationship with whoever you turn to for financial help. Good help or bad help is not a function of the type or size of organization the individual works with or even of how the help gets paid – it's a function of what they do for you and how they do it - so that's what you've got to investigate. In doing so, I encourage you to be open-minded but certainly ask tough questions, to which you're entitled to get answers that satisfy any concerns you have.

It's a fine starting point to have someone you trust and respect recommend an advisor to you but that advisor still should pass muster based on the following criteria (and, if you find that they don't, you might help that person you trust and respect see the light):

1. What are they going to do for you and how are they going to do it? Specifically, do they have a process/model and ability to comprehensively review all aspects of your financial world (i.e., all the things discussed in this book)? You're not going to do that and an advisor whose scope is too narrow (because that's how they get paid – as in an estate attorney, a stock broker, a life insurance person, a CPA) isn't going to do it either.

2. Will they assist you in making integrated and strategic decisions with a view toward protecting you, your family and your money and putting you in a position to have the most robust retirement possible or are they primarily about selling you some product or another?

3. Are they well-versed in all of the relevant financial disciplines – not that they necessarily know each one to the nth degree but enough to serve as your CFO and knowledgeably lead, assess and integrate your decision making, taking charge of other experts on your behalf as necessary?

4. Are they willing to "invest" in the relationship with you – for instance, will they spend meaningful thought and time with you getting matters in your financial world right for which they aren't or can't be compensated – <u>e.g.</u>, working on getting your mortgage refinanced, your wills done, etc.?

5. Will there be a regular, ongoing relationship where there will be adjustments made and future needs, opportunities or challenges addressed (without regard to whether they're going to get paid again)? For this type of relationship to achieve its greatest potential for the client, it needs to be one that is specifically intended and organized to be a lifetime one.

6. On a personal level, do you feel <u>comfortable</u> with whoever you'd be dealing with – and it couldn't hurt if you actually even <u>like</u> them because you're going to have a long-term and close relationship. Further, on a more technical level, do they have the credentials to reinforce the comfort you have with them? Specifically, I would suggest that a good standard is whether they and their firm are Registered Investment Advisors. "RIAs", as they're called, are subject to the highest legal/fiduciary standard of care in the business.

7. And, of course, is what they know and do the *common* or the *uncommon*? (I think this book should prepare you well to ask plenty of "trick" questions to

assess that – <u>e.g.</u>, "How much should I save in my 401(k)?" or "Isn't it always a good idea to buy term and invest the difference?" and so on.)

I truly hope the above information will help put you on a path to finding someone to work with who can help to further your financial success in powerful and uncommon ways.